하루 10분 초등영단어 따라쓰기

3~6학년 영단어 한 권으로 끝내기

키즈키즈 교육연구소 지음

미래주니어

차례

머리말

쉽게 읽고, 쉽게 암기하는 〈하루 10분 초등 영단어 따라쓰기〉

영어 공부의 기초는 단어 익히기에서 시작하며, 발음 기호 공부가 선행되어야 합니다. 단어를 읽을 줄 알아야 암기할 수 있고, 단어가 익숙해져야 쓰기와 말하기가 자연스럽게 이어집니다. 그러나 단어를 잘 읽지 못하니 결국은 영어에 대한 흥미까지 떨어지게 됩니다. 발음 기호를 알면 영단어를 쉽게 읽을 수 있습니다. 또한 영어사전을 활용해 스스로 모르는 단어를 찾아 자기주도적인 학습이 가능해지며, 영어 공부에 흥미를 가질 수 있습니다.

〈하루 10분 초등 영단어 따라쓰기〉는 발음 기호와 함께 원음과 가깝게 한글 발음도 표기하여 누구나 영단어를 쉽게 익히고 영어 자신감을 키울 수 있습니다. 하루에 10개 영단어를 따라 쓰면 100일이면 초등 필수 영단어 1000개를 익힐 수 있습니다. 본문을 3학년부터 6학년까지 학년별로 분류하여 난이도와 각자의 학습 역량에 맞게 공부하면 됩니다. 하루 10분씩 매일 매일 꾸준히 따라 쓰며 초등 영어의 기초를 탄탄히 다지세요!

초등 필수 영단어 1000개를 한 권으로 익혀요!

발음 기호 읽는 법

영어는 한글과 다르게 하나의 알파벳이 여러 가지 소리를 가지고 있습니다. 주로 모음 글자가 여러 발음을 가지고 있으며, 발음 기호를 익히고 읽는 연습을 하다 보면 스펠링만 보고서도 단어를 읽을 수 있게 됩니다. 또한 악센트가 있는 단어도 있어서 악센트 표시가 있는 부분은 강하게 읽어야 합니다.

[a] 아
우리말의 [아]보다 입을 더 크게 벌리고 목청이 떨리는 듯한 깊은 소리를 냅니다.

    clock [klak 클락] 시계
    hot [hat 핫] 뜨거운

[e] 에
우리말 [에]보다 입술을 옆으로 최대한 벌려서 소리를 냅니다.

    egg [eg 에ㄱ] 달걀
    empty [émpti 엠프티] 비어 있는

[i] 이
입술을 최대한 옆으로 벌리고 [이] 소리를 냅니다.

    in [in 인] ~ 안에
    if [if 이프] 만약 ~라면

[o] 오
입술을 동그랗게 만들어 부드럽고 맑게 [오] 소리를 냅니다.

    old [ould 오울드] 늙은
    open [óupən 오우펀] 열다

[u] 우
입술은 동그랗게 내밀고 혀는 안쪽으로 당기면서 [우] 소리를 냅니다.

    bowl [boul 보울] 그릇
    wood [wud 우드] 나무

[ə] 어
입술을 위아래로 조금 벌린 상태로 [어] 소리를 냅니다.

    again [əgén 어겐] 다시
    ago [əgóu 어고우] ~ 전에

[ʌ] 어
[ə]와 발음은 같지만, [ə]는 약한 악센트에 사용되며 [ʌ]는 강한 악센트에 사용됩니다.

    sun [sʌn 썬] 해
    bucket [bʌ́kit 버킷] 양동이

[ɔ] 오
입술을 동그랗게 만들어 우리말 [오]보다 더 입 안쪽에서 소리를 냅니다.

    all [ɔːl 오-ㄹ] 모든
    boy [bɔi 보이] 소년

[ɛ] 에

입을 크게 벌리고 [에]라고 소리를 냅니다.

air [ɛər 에어] 공기
hair [hɛər 헤어] 머리카락

[æ] 애

입을 크게 벌리고 목에서 나는 소리로 [애]라고 소리를 냅니다.

act [ækt 액트] 행동하다
and [ænd 앤드] 그리고

[d] 드

혀를 윗니 안쪽에 대고 있다가 떼면서 짧게 [드]라고 소리를 냅니다.

draw [drɔ: 드로-] 그리다
dress [dres 드레스] 드레스

[t] 트

혀를 윗니 끝에 대고 있다가 떼면서 강하게 [트]라고 소리를 냅니다.

train [trein 트레인] 기차
tree [tri: 트리-] 나무

[n] 느

혀끝을 윗니와 아랫니로 살짝 물고 있다가 떼면서 짧게 [느] 소리를 냅니다.

new [nu: 뉴-] 새로운
nose [nouz 노우즈] 코

[l] 르

혀끝으로 입천장을 누르면서 [을] 소리를 내는 기분으로 [르]을 소리 냅니다.

lion [láiən 라이언] 사자
look [luk 룩] 보다

[r] 르

혀끝을 입천장에 대지 않고 둥글게 말아서 [르]을 소리 냅니다.

rice [rais 라이스] 쌀
red [red 레드] 빨간색

[f] 프 / [v] 브

[f]는 윗니로 아랫입술 안쪽을 눌렀다 떼면서 [프] 소리를 냅니다. [v]는 위와 같은 방법으로 [브] 소리를 냅니다.

face [feis 페이스] 얼굴
voice [vɔis 보이스] 목소리

[m] 므 / [b] 브 / [p] 프

입술을 다물었다 급하게 옆으로 벌리면서 [m]은 [므], [b]는 [브], [p]는 [프] 소리를 냅니다.

map [mæp 맵] 지도
book [buk 북] 책
pig [pig 피그] 돼지

[k] 크 / [g] 그 / [h] 흐

혀를 안쪽으로 올려 입천장 가까이에서 [k]는 [크], [g]는 [그], [h]는 [흐] 소리를 냅니다.

kind [kaind 카인드] 친절한
girl [gə:rl 거-얼] 소녀
help [help 헬프] 돕다

[s] 스 / [z] 즈

입술을 최대한 옆으로 벌린 상태로 [s]는 [스], [z]는 [즈] 소리를 냅니다.

ski [ski: 스키-] 스키
zoo [zu: 주-] 동물원

[ʃ] 쉬 / [ʒ] 지

입술을 둥글게 모아 앞으로 내민 상태로 [ʃ]
는 [쉬], [ʒ]는 [지] 소리를 냅니다.

- shoes [ʃuːz 슈-즈] 신발
- usually [juːʒuəli 유-주얼리] 보통

[dʒ] 쥐 / [tʃ] 취

혀를 윗니 안쪽에 대고 [dʒ]는 [쥐], [tʃ]는
[취] 소리를 냅니다.

- village [vílidʒ 빌리쥐] 마을
- beach [biːtʃ 비-취] 해변

[θ] 쓰 / [ð] 드

윗니와 아랫니로 혀 중간을 가볍게 물었다
가 안쪽으로 들이밀면서 [θ]는 [쓰], [ð]는
[드] 소리를 냅니다.

- health [helθ 헬쓰] 건강
- with [wið 위드] ~와 함께

[ŋ] 응

코로 공기를 내보내며 [응] 소리를 냅니다.

- wing [wiŋ 윙] 날개
- king [kiŋ 킹] 왕

발음 기호를 익히면
영단어를 쉽게 읽고
쉽게 암기할 수 있어요!

3학년
필수 영단어
따라쓰기

air
[ɛər] 에어

공기

air air air air air

airplane
[ɛ́ərplèin] 에어플레인

비행기

airplane airplane airplane

airport
[ɛ́ərpɔ́ːrt] 에어포ー트

공항

airport airport airport

album
[ǽlbəm] 앨범

앨범

album album album

animal
[ǽnəməl] 애너멀

동물

animal animal animal

예술가

ant
[ænt] 앤트
개미

ant ant ant ant ant

apple
[ǽpl] 애플
사과

apple apple apple apple

arm
[ɑ:rm] 아-암
팔

arm arm arm arm arm

art
[ɑ:rt] 아-트
예술, 미술

art art art art art

artist
[ɑ́:rtist] 아-티스트
예술가

artist artist artist artist

baby
[béibi] 베이비
아기

baby baby baby baby

back
[bæk] 백
뒤, 등

back back back back

bad
[bæd] 배드
나쁜

bad bad bad bad

bag
[bæg] 백
가방

bag bag bag bag bag

ball
[bɔːl] 보-ㄹ
공

ball ball ball ball ball

banana
[bənǽnə] 버내너

바나나

banana banana banana

bank
[bæŋk] 뱅크

은행

bank bank bank bank

bath
[bæθ] 배쓰

목욕

bath bath bath bath

bathroom
[bǽθrùːm] 배쓰룸

욕실

bathroom bathroom bathroom

bear
[bɛər] 베어

곰

bear bear bear bear

bed
[bed] 베드
침대

bed bed bed bed bed

bee
[bi:] 비-
벌

bee bee bee bee bee

beef
[bi:f] 비-프
소고기

beef beef beef beef

bell
[bel] 벨
벨, 종

bell bell bell bell bell

big
[big] 빅
큰

big big big big big

bird
[bəːrd] 버-드

새

bird bird bird bird bird

birthday
[bə́ːrθdèi] 버-쓰데이

생일

birthday birthday birthday

black
[blæk] 블랙

검은색

black black black black

blue
[bluː] 블루-

파란색

blue blue blue blue blue

boat
[bout] 보우트

배, 보트

boat boat boat boat

body
[bádi] 바디

몸

body body body body

book
[buk] 북

책

book book book book

box
[baks] 박스

상자

box box box box box

boy
[bɔi] 보이

남자 아이, 소년

boy boy boy boy boy

brother
[brʌðər] 브러더

형, 오빠, 남동생

brother brother brother

brown
[braun] 브라운

갈색

brown　brown　brown

bus
[bʌs] 버스

버스

bus　bus　bus　bus　bus

bye
[bai] 바이

잘 가, 안녕

bye　bye　bye　bye　bye

cake
[keik] 케익

케이크

cake　cake　cake　cake

call
[kɔːl] 코ー르

전화하다

call　call　call　call　call

camera

[kǽmərə] 캐머러

카메라

camera camera camera

candy

[kǽndi] 캔디

사탕

candy candy candy candy

cap

[kæp] 캡

모자

cap cap cap cap cap

car

[kɑːr] 카-

자동차

car car car car car

card

[kɑːrd] 카-드

카드

card card card card card

carrot
[kǽrət] 캐럿

당근

carrot   carrot   carrot   carrot

cat
[kæt] 캔

고양이

cat   cat   cat   cat   cat

chair
[tʃɛər] 체어

의자

chair   chair   chair   chair

chicken
[tʃíkin] 치킨

닭

chicken   chicken   chicken

child
[tʃaild] 차일드

아이, 어린이

child   child   child   child

city
[síti] 시티
도시

city city city city city

clock
[klɑk] 클락
시계

clock clock clock clock

coat
[kout] 코우트
외투

coat coat coat coat coat

cold
[kould] 코울드
차가운, 추운

cold cold cold cold cold

color
[kʌlər] 컬러
색깔

color color color color color

cook

[kuk] 쿡

요리하다

cook cook cook cook

cookie

[kúki] 쿠키

쿠키

cookie cookie cookie

cow

[kau] 카우

소

cow cow cow cow cow

crayon

[kréiən] 크레이언

크레용

crayon crayon crayon

cup

[kʌp] 컵

컵

cup cup cup cup cup

dad
[dæd] 대드
아빠

dad dad dad dad dad

desk
[desk] 데스크
책상

desk desk desk desk desk

diary
[dáiəri] 다이어리
일기

diary diary diary diary

dinner
[dínər] 디너
저녁 식사

dinner dinner dinner

dish
[diʃ] 디쉬
접시

dish dish dish dish dish

doctor
[dάktər] 닥터
의사

doctor   doctor   doctor

dog
[dɔ:g] 도-ㄱ
개

dog   dog   dog   dog   dog

doll
[dɑl] 달
인형

doll   doll   doll   doll   doll

door
[dɔ:r] 도-
문

door   door   door   door

down
[daun] 다운
아래로

down   down   down   down

dress
[dres] 드레스

드레스, 옷

dress　dress　dress　dress

duck
[dʌk] 덕

오리

duck　duck　duck　duck

ear
[iər] 이어

귀

ear　ear　ear　ear　ear

egg
[eg] 에ㄱ

달걀

egg　egg　egg　egg　egg

elephant
[éləfənt] 엘러펀트

코끼리

elephant　elephant　elephant

evening
[íːvniŋ] 이-브닝
저녁

evening   evening   evening

eye
[ai] 아이
눈

eye   eye   eye   eye   eye

face
[feis] 페이스
얼굴

face face face face face

family
[fǽməli] 패멀리
가족

family   family   family

farm
[fɑːrm] 팜-
농장

farm   farm   farm   farm

farmer

[fάːrmər] 파ー머

농부

farmer　farmer　farmer

father

[fάːðər] 파ー더

아버지

father　father　father

fish

[fiʃ] 피쉬

물고기

fish　fish　fish　fish　fish

flower

[fláuər] 플라워

꽃

flower　flower　flower

fly

[flai] 플라이

날다

fly　fly　fly　fly　fly

foot
[fut] 풀

발

foot   foot   foot   foot

football
[fútbɔ̀:l] 풋볼-

축구

football   football   football

friend
[frend] 프렌드

친구

friend   friend   friend

frog
[frɔ:g] 프로-ㄱ

개구리

frog   frog   frog   frog

fruit
[fru:t] 프루-트

과일

fruit   fruit   fruit   fruit

game
[geim] 게임

게임, 경기

game game game game

garden
[gá:rdn] 가-든

정원

garden garden garden

gift
[gift] 기프트

선물

gift gift gift gift

girl
[gə:rl] 거-얼

소녀

girl girl girl girl

good
[gud] 굳

좋은

good good good good

grape
[greip] 그레이프

포도

grape   grape   grape

great
[greit] 그레이트

위대한, 큰

great   great   great   great

hair
[hɛər] 헤어

머리카락

hair   hair   hair   hair

hand
[hænd] 핸드

손

hand   hand   hand   hand

happy
[hǽpi] 해피

행복한

happy   happy   happy

hat
[hæt] 햍
모자

hat hat hat hat hat

hello
[helóu] 헬로우
안녕하세요

hello hello hello hello

here
[hiər] 히어
여기

here here here here

hi
[hai] 하이
안녕

hi hi hi hi hi

hill
[hil] 힐
언덕

hill hill hill hill hill

home
[houm] 호움
집

home home home home

homework
[houmwə̀:rk] 호움워-크
숙제

homework homework

horse
[hɔːrs] 호-스
말

horse horse horse horse

hospital
[háspitl] 하스피틀
병원

hospital hospital hospital

hot
[hɑt] 핱
뜨거운, 더운

hot hot hot hot hot

hotel
[houtél] 호우텔
호텔

hotel hotel hotel hotel

house
[haus] 하우스
집

house house house

hungry
[hʌ́ŋgri] 헝그리
배고픈

hungry hungry hungry

hurry
[hə́:ri] 허-리
서두르다

hurry hurry hurry hurry

I
[ai] 아이
나

ice
[ais] 아이스

얼음

ice   ice   ice   ice   ice

ice cream
[áis krì:m] 아이스 크리-ㅁ

아이스크림

ice cream   ice cream

idea
[aidí:ə] 아이디-어

생각, 아이디어

idea   idea   idea   idea

juice
[dʒu:s] 쥬-스

주스

juice   juice   juice   juice

jump
[dʒʌmp] 점프

뛰다, 점프하다

jump   jump   jump   jump

key
[ki:] 키-

열쇠

key key key key key

kid
[kid] 키드

아이

kid kid kid kid kid

king
[kiŋ] 킹

왕

king king king king

lady
[léidi] 레이디

여성, 숙녀

lady lady lady lady

like
[laik] 라이크

좋아하다

like like like like like

lion
[láiən] 라이언
사자

lion   lion   lion   lion   lion

love
[lʌv] 러브
사랑, 사랑하다

love   love   love   love   love

lunch
[lʌntʃ] 런취
점심 식사

lunch   lunch   lunch   lunch

man
[mæn] 맨
(성인) 남자

man   man   man   man   man

map
[mæp] 맵
지도

map   map   map   map   map

meat
[mi:t] 미-트
고기

meat meat meat meat

milk
[milk] 밀크
우유

milk milk milk milk

mirror
[mírər] 미러
거울

mirror mirror mirror mirror

mom
[mam] 맘
엄마

mom mom mom mom

money
[mʌ́ni] 머니
돈

money money money money

monkey

[mʌ́ŋki] 멍키

원숭이

monkey monkey monkey

moon

[muːn] 무ー느

달

moon moon moon moon

mother

[mʌ́ðər] 머더

어머니

mother mother mother

mouth

[mauθ] 마우쓰

입

mouth mouth mouth mouth

movie

[múːvi] 무ー비

영화

movie movie movie movie

music
[mjú:zik] 뮤-직
음악

music music music music

name
[neim] 네임
이름

name name name name

no
[nou] 노우
없다, 아니다

no no no no no

nose
[nouz] 노우즈
코

nose nose nose nose

note
[nout] 노우트
메모

note note note note

notebook

[nóutbùk] 노우트북

노트, 공책

notebook   notebook

oil

[ɔil] 오일

기름

oil   oil   oil   oil   oil

OK

[óukèi] 오우케이

좋아

OK   OK   OK   OK   OK

onion

[ʌ́njən] 어년

양파

onion   onion   onion   onion

open

[óupən] 오우펀

열다

open   open   open   open

orange
[ɔ́:rindʒ] 오-린쥐
오렌지

orange   orange   orange

paint
[peint] 페인트
그리다, 페인트

paint   paint   paint   paint

pants
[pænts] 팬츠
바지

pants   pants   pants   pants

paper
[péipər] 페이퍼
종이

paper   paper   paper

park
[pɑːrk] 파-크
공원

park   park   park   park

party
[páːrti] 파―티

파티

party   party   party   party

pear
[pɛər] 페어

배

pear   pear   pear   pear

pen
[pen] 펜

펜

pen   pen   pen   pen   pen

pencil
[pénsl] 펜슬

연필

pencil   pencil   pencil

pencil case
[pénsl keis] 펜슬 케이스

필통

pencil case   pencil case

photo
[fóutou] 포우토우
사진

photo photo photo photo

piano
[piǽnou] 피애노우
피아노

piano piano piano piano

pig
[pig] 피그
돼지

pig pig pig pig pig

plane
[plein] 플레인
비행기

plane plane plane plane

play
[plei] 플레이
놀다

play play play play

point
[pɔint] 포인트

요점, 가리키다

point point point point

police
[pəlíːs] 펄리-스

경찰

police police police police

potato
[pətéitou] 퍼테이토우

감자

potato potato potato

pretty
[príti] 프리티

예쁜, 귀여운

pretty pretty pretty pretty

prince
[prins] 프린스

왕자

prince prince prince prince

princess

[prínsis] 프린시스

공주

princess   princess   princess

queen

[kwi:n] 퀴-ㄴ

여왕

queen   queen   queen

rabbit

[rǽbit] 래빝

토끼

rabbit   rabbit   rabbit   rabbit

radio

[réidiòu] 레이디오우

라디오

radio   radio   radio   radio

rain

[rein] 레인

비

rain   rain   rain   rain

rainbow

[réinbòu] 레인보우

무지개

rainbow rainbow rainbow

rice

[rais] 라이스

쌀, 밥

rice rice rice rice rice

ring

[riŋ] 링

반지

ring ring ring ring ring

river

[rívər] 리버

강

river river river river

road

[roud] 로우드

도로, 길

road road road road

robot
[róubət] 로우벗
로봇

robot robot robot robot

room
[ru:m] 루-ㅁ
방

room room room room

ruler
[rú:lər] 룰-러
자

ruler ruler ruler ruler

salt
[sɔ:lt] 솔-트
소금

salt salt salt salt salt

school
[sku:l] 스쿠-ㄹ
학교

school school school

sea
[siː] 씨-
바다

sea sea sea sea sea

ship
[ʃip] 쉽
배

ship ship ship ship ship

shirt
[ʃəːrt] 셔-트
셔츠

shirt shirt shirt shirt

shoes
[ʃuːz] 슈-즈
신발

shoes shoes shoes shoes

shop
[ʃap] 샵
상점, 가게

shop shop shop shop

sing
[siŋ] 싱
노래하다

sing sing sing sing sing

singer
[síŋər] 씽어
가수

singer singer singer singer

sister
[sístər] 씨스터
언니, 누나, 여동생

sister sister sister sister

skate
[skeit] 스케이트
스케이트

skate skate skate skate

ski
[ski:] 스키–
스키

ski ski ski ski ski

sky
[skai] 스카이

하늘

sky   sky   sky   sky   sky

small
[smɔːl] 스모-ㄹ

작은

small   small   small   small

smile
[smail] 스마일

미소

smile   smile   smile   smile

snow
[snou] 스노우

눈

snow   snow   snow   snow

snowman
[snóumæn] 스노우맨

눈사람

snowman   snowman   snowman

son
[sʌn] 썬
아들

son son son son son

song
[sɔ́:ŋ] 쏭
노래

song song song song

sorry
[sɑ́ri] 싸리
미안한

sorry sorry sorry sorry

star
[stɑ:r] 스타-
별

star star star star star

stop
[stɑp] 스탑
멈추다

stop stop stop stop

store
[stɔːr] 스토-

가게, 상점

store   store   store   store

story
[stɔ́ːri] 스토-리

이야기

story   story   story   story

student
[stjúːdənt] 스튜-던트

학생

student   student   student

sugar
[ʃúgər] 슈거

설탕

sugar   sugar   sugar   sugar

sun
[sʌn] 썬

해, 태양

sun   sun   sun   sun   sun

sweet
[swi:t] 스위-ㅌ
달콤한

sweet sweet sweet sweet

swim
[swim] 스윔
수영하다

swim swim swim swim

table
[téibl] 테이블
탁자

table table table table

taxi
[tǽksi] 택시
택시

taxi taxi taxi taxi

tea
[ti:] 티-
차

tea tea tea tea tea

teach
[ti:tʃ] 티-취

가르치다

teach teach teach teach

teacher
[tíːtʃər] 티-쳐

선생님

teacher teacher teacher

textbook
[tékstbùk] 텍스트북

교과서

textbook textbook textbook

thank
[θæŋk] 쌩크

감사하다

thank thank thank thank

that
[ðæt] 댇

저것

that that that that

this

[ðis] 디스

이것

this this this this this

time

[taim] 타임

시간

time time time time

tomato

[təméitou] 터메이토우

토마토

tomato tomato tomato

too

[tu:] 투-

또한, 너무

too too too too too

tower

[táuər] 타워

탑

tower tower tower tower

toy
[tɔi] 토이

장난감

toy toy toy toy toy

train
[trein] 트레인

기차

train train train train

tree
[tri:] 트리–

나무

tree tree tree tree

up
[ʌp] 업

위로

up up up up up

violin
[vàiəlín] 바이얼린

바이올린

violin violin violin violin

wait
[weit] 웨이트
기다리다

wait wait wait wait

wall
[wɔ:l] 월-
벽

wall wall wall wall

wash
[wɑʃ] 와쉬
씻다

wash wash wash wash

watch
[wɑtʃ] 와취
손목시계, 보다

watch watch watch watch

water
[wɔ́:tər] 워-터
물

water water water water

watermelon
[wɔ́:tərmèlən] 워-터멜런

수박

watermelon watermelon

welcome
[wélkəm] 웰컴

환영하다

welcome welcome welcome

wind
[wind] 윈드

바람

wind wind wind wind

window
[wíndou] 윈도우

창문

window window window

wolf
[wulf] 울프

늑대

wolf wolf wolf wolf

wood
[wud] 우드

나무, 목재

wood wood wood wood

word
[wəːrd] 워-드

단어, 낱말

word word word word

work
[wəːrk] 웍-

일하다

work work work work

world
[wəːrld] 워-르드

세계, 세상

world world world world

wow
[wau] 와우

(감탄사) 야, 와

wow wow wow wow

동물원

yard
[jɑːrd] 야-드

마당, 뜰

yard   yard   yard   yard

yes
[jes] 예스

네, 그래

yes   yes   yes   yes   yes

you
[juː] 유-

너

you   you   you   you   you

zebra
[zíːbrə] 지-브러

얼룩말

zebra   zebra   zebra   zebra

zoo
[zuː] 주-

동물원

zoo   zoo   zoo   zoo   zoo

재미있는 영단어 퀴즈

1 아래 그림을 보고 빈칸을 채워 영단어를 완성하세요.

1) du___   2) ___plane   3) ca___ot

4) rain___   5) p___cil   6) tr___

2 아래 보기에서 알맞은 우리말을 찾아 쓰세요.

> **보기**
>
> 포도   의사   농장   동물   병원   어린이

1) animal _____   4) doctor _____

2) farm _____   5) grape _____

3) hospital _____   6) child _____

정답

2. 1) animal 동물 2) farm 농장 3) hospital 병원 4) doctor 의사 5) grape 포도 6) child 어린이

1. 1) duck 2) airplane 3) carrot 4) rainbow 5) pencil 6) tree

58

3 우리말에 맞게 영단어를 바르게 써 보세요.

e o m h ➡ 집 home

1) w a r e t
물 _____

4) i k n g
왕 _____

2) a r p t y
파티 _____

5) s l i e m
미소 _____

3) s t y r o
이야기 _____

6) a m p
지도 _____

4 영단어에 알맞은 우리말을 줄로 연결하세요.

1) bank ·   · 은행

2) chair ·   · 농부

3) farmer ·   · 공항

4) airport ·   · 의자

정답

4. 1) bank 은행 2) chair 의자 3) farmer 농부 4) airport 공항

3. 1) water 물 2) party 파티 3) story 이야기 4) king 왕 5) smile 미소 6) map 지도

5 우리말에 알맞은 영단어를 쓰고 퍼즐을 완성하세요.

힌트

family   birthday   piano
nose   school   police

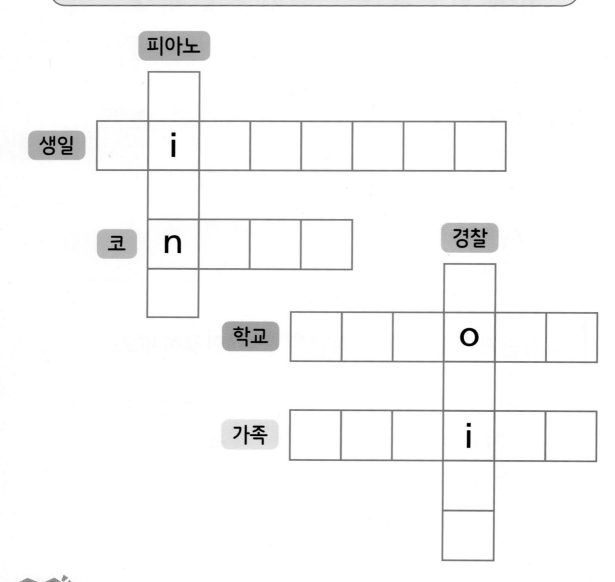

피아노

생일 | i

코 | n

경찰

학교 | o

가족 | i

4학년
필수 영단어
따라쓰기

afternoon

[æftərnúːn] 앱터누운

오후

afternoon afternoon

age

[eidʒ] 에이쥐

나이

age age age age age

all

[ɔːl] 오-ㄹ

모든

all all all all all

angry

[ǽŋgri] 앵그리

화난

angry angry angry

army

[áːrmi] 아-미

군대

army army army army

balloon
[bəlúːn] 벌루-ㄴ

풍선

balloon   balloon   balloon

base
[beis] 베이스

기초, 토대

base   base   base   base

basket
[bǽskit] 배스킽

바구니

basket   basket   basket

bat
[bæt] 뱉

박쥐, 방망이

bat   bat   bat   bat   bat

beach
[biːtʃ] 비-취

해변

beach   beach   beach   beach

beautiful

[bjúːtifəl] 뷰-티펄

아름다운

beautiful beautiful

bedroom

[bédrùːm] 베드루-ㅁ

침실

bedroom bedroom

belt

[belt] 벨트

허리띠

belt belt belt belt

bike

[baik] 바이크

자전거

bike bike bike bike

block

[blɑk] 블락

블록

block block block block

blouse
[blaus] 블라우스

블라우스

blouse   blouse   blouse

bookcase
[búkkèis] 북케이스

책장

bookcase   bookcase

boots
[bu:ts] 부-츠

부츠, 장화

boots   boots   boots   boots

bottle
[bátl] 바틀

병

bottle   bottle   bottle   bottle

bowl
[boul] 보울

그릇

bowl   bowl   bowl   bowl

bread
[bred] 브레드

빵

bread   bread   bread

breakfast
[brékfəst] 브렉퍼스트

아침 식사

breakfast   breakfast

bridge
[bridʒ] 브리쥐

다리

bridge   bridge   bridge

busy
[bízi] 비지

바쁜

busy   busy   busy   busy

butter
[bʌ́tər] 버터

버터

butter   butter   butter   butter

button
[bʌ́tn] 버튼
단추

button   button   button

buy
[bai] 바이
사다

buy   buy   buy   buy   buy

camping
[kǽmpiŋ] 캠핑
캠핑, 야영

camping   camping   camping

can
[kæn] 캔
할 수 있다

can   can   can   can   can

candle
[kǽndl] 캔들
양초

candle   candle   candle

case
[keis] 케이스
상자, 통

case case case case case

chalk
[tʃɔːk] 초-크
분필

chalk chalk chalk chalk

cheese
[tʃiːz] 치-즈
치즈

cheese cheese cheese

chocolate
[tʃɔ́ːkəlit] 초커릿
초콜릿

chocolate chocolate

Christmas
[krísməs] 크리스머스
크리스마스

Christmas Christmas

church
[tʃəːrtʃ] 처-취

교회

church   church   church

class
[klæs] 클래스

학급, 수업

class   class   class   class

classmate
[klǽsmèit] 클래스메이트

동급생, 반 친구

classmate   classmate

classroom
[klǽsrùːm] 클래스룸

교실

classroom   classroom

clean
[kliːn] 클리-ㄴ

청소하다, 깨끗한

clean   clean   clean   clean

close
[klouz] 클로우즈
닫다

close close close close

cloud
[klaud] 클라우드
구름

cloud cloud cloud cloud

cloudy
[kláudi] 클라우디
구름 낀

cloudy cloudy cloudy

coin
[kɔin] 코인
동전

coin coin coin coin coin

come
[kʌm] 컴
오다

come come come come

computer

[kəmpjúːtər] 컴퓨터

컴퓨터

computer   computer

concert

[kánsəːrt] 칸서트

공연

concert   concert   concert

cool

[kuːl] 쿠－ㄹ

시원한

cool   cool   cool   cool

copy

[kápi] 카피

복사, 모방

copy   copy   copy   copy

corn

[kɔːrn] 콘－

옥수수

corn   corn   corn   corn

cross
[krɔːs] 크로-스

건너다, 가로지르다

cross cross cross cross

cry
[krai] 크라이

울다

cry cry cry cry cry

cut
[kʌt] 커트

자르다

cut cut cut cut cut

cute
[kjuːt] 큐-트

귀여운

cute cute cute cute

dance
[dæns] 댄스

춤추다

dance dance dance dance

dark

[dɑ:rk] 다-크

어두운

dark dark dark dark

date

[deit] 데이트

날짜

date date date date

deer

[diər] 디어

사슴

deer deer deer deer

dentist

[déntist] 덴티스트

치과 의사

dentist dentist dentist

die

[dai] 다이

죽다

die die die die die

do
[du:] 두-

~하다

do do do do do

double
[dʌbl] 더블

두 배의

double double double

draw
[drɔ:] 드로-

그리다

draw draw draw draw

dream
[dri:m] 드리-ㅁ

꿈, 희망

dream dream dream dream

drink
[driŋk] 드링크

마시다

drink drink drink drink

drive
[draiv] 드라이브
운전하다

drive drive drive drive

driver
[dráivər] 드라이버
운전사

driver driver driver driver

dry
[drai] 드라이
마른, 말리다

dry dry dry dry dry

earth
[ə:rθ] 어-쓰
지구, 땅, 흙

earth earth earth earth

east
[i:st] 이-스트
동쪽

east east east east

easy
[íːzi] 이-지
쉬운

easy   easy   easy   easy

eat
[iːt] 이-트
먹다

eat   eat   eat   eat   eat

end
[end] 엔드
끝, 끝내다

end   end   end   end   end

English
[íŋgliʃ] 잉글리쉬
영어

English   English   English

ABC

enjoy
[indʒɔ́i] 인조이
즐기다

enjoy   enjoy   enjoy   enjoy

eraser
[iréisər] 이레이서

지우개

eraser eraser eraser eraser

event
[ivént] 이벤트

행사, 이벤트

event event event event

everyone
[évriwʌ́n] 에브리원

모든 사람

everyone everyone

fact
[fækt] 팩트

사실

fact fact fact fact

fat
[fæt] 팯

살찐, 뚱뚱한

fat fat fat fat fat

film
[film] 필름
필름, 영화

film film film film film

fire
[faiər] 파이어
불

fire fire fire fire fire

food
[fu:d] 푸-드
음식

food food food food

for
[fɔ́:r] 포-
~을 위해

for for for for for

fork
[fɔ:rk] 포-크
포크

fork fork fork fork fork

fox
[fɑ:ks] 팍스

여우

fox fox fox fox fox

free
[fri:] 프리-

자유로운

free free free free

fun
[fʌn] 펀

재미, 재미있는

fun fun fun fun fun

funny
[fʌ́ni] 퍼니

우스운, 웃기는

funny funny funny funny

gas
[gæs] 개스

가스, 기체

gas gas gas gas gas

gate
[geit] 게이트
문, 대문

gate gate gate gate

giraffe
[dʒəræf] 저래프
기린

giraffe giraffe giraffe

glass
[glæs] 글래스
유리, 유리컵

glass glass glass glass

go
[gou] 고우
가다

go go go go go

gold
[gould] 고울드
금색

gold gold gold gold

goldfish
[góuldfiʃ] 고울드피쉬

금붕어

goldfish goldfish goldfish

gray
[grei] 그레이

회색

gray gray gray gray

green
[gri:n] 그리-ㄴ

초록색

green green green green

group
[gru:p] 그룹

그룹, 단체

group group group group

hall
[hɔ:l] 호-ㄹ

홀, 집회장

hall hall hall hall hall

have
[hæv] 해브
가지다, 먹다

have have have have

he
[hi:] 히-
그

he he he he he

hear
[hiər] 히어
듣다

hear hear hear hear

heart
[hɑːrt] 하-트
심장, 가슴

heart heart heart heart

heat
[hiːt] 히-트
열, 더위

heat heat heat heat

help
[help] 헬프
돕다

help   help   help   help

hen
[hen] 헨
암탉

hen   hen   hen   hen   hen

high
[hai] 하이
높은

high   high   high   high

in
[in] 인
~안에

in   in   in   in   in

it
[it] 잍
그것

it   it   it   it   it

job
[dʒɑb] 잡
직업

job job job job job

kill
[kil] 킬
죽이다

kill kill kill kill kill

kind
[kaind] 카인드
친절한

kind kind kind kind

kitchen
[kítʃin] 키췬
주방

kitchen kitchen kitchen

knee
[ni:] 니-
무릎

knee knee knee knee

know
[nou] 노우

알다

know　know　know　know

Korea
[kərí:ə] 커리-어

한국, 대한민국

Korea　Korea　Korea

lake
[leik] 레이크

호수

lake　lake　lake　lake

lamp
[læmp] 램프

램프, 전등

lamp　lamp　lamp　lamp

land
[lænd] 랜드

땅, 육지

land　land　land　land

late
[leit] 레이트

늦은

late late late late late

leg
[leg] 렉

다리

leg leg leg leg leg

let's
[lets] 렏츠

~하자

let's let's let's let's let's

letter
[létər] 레터

편지

letter letter letter letter

library
[láibrèri] 라이브레리

도서관

library library library library

line
[lain] 라인
줄

line line line line line

lip
[lip] 립
입술

lip lip lip lip lip

list
[list] 리스트
목록

list list list list list

living room
[lívɪŋ rùːm] 리빙 루ㅡㅁ
거실

living room living room

long
[lɔːŋ] 로ㅡㅇ
긴

long long long long

look
[luk] 룩
보다

look look look look

low
[lou] 로우
낮은

low low low low low

mail
[meil] 메일
우편

mail mail mail mail

make
[meik] 메이크
만들다

make make make make

many
[méni] 메니
(수가) 많은

many many many many

market
[mάːrkit] 마-킽

시장

market   market   market

marry
[mǽri] 매리

결혼하다

marry marry marry marry

meet
[miːt] 미-트

만나다

meet   meet   meet   meet

meeting
[míːtiŋ] 미-팅

만남, 회의

meeting   meeting   meeting

minus
[máinəs] 마이너스

빼기, 빼다

minus minus minus minus

morning

[mɔ́ːrniŋ] 모-닝

아침

morning   morning   morning

mouse

[maus] 마우스

쥐

mouse   mouse   mouse   mouse

much

[mʌtʃ] 머취

(양이) 많은

much   much   much   much

nature

[néitʃər] 네이쳐

자연

nature   nature   nature   nature

neck

[nek] 넥

목

neck   neck   neck   neck

new
[nu:] 뉴-
새로운

new new new new new

news
[nu:z] 뉴-즈
뉴스, 보도

news news news news

newspaper
[núːzpèipər] 뉴-즈페이퍼
신문

newspaper newspaper

next
[nekst] 넥스트
다음의, 옆의

next next next next

nice
[nais] 나이스
좋은

nice nice nice nice

north
[nɔːrθ] 노-쓰
북쪽

north   north   north   north

now
[nau] 나우
지금, 현재

now   now   now   now   now

number
[nʌ́mbər] 넘버
숫자

number   number   number

136

nurse
[nəːrs] 너-스
간호사

nurse   nurse   nurse   nurse

ocean
[óuʃən] 오우션
바다, 대양

ocean   ocean   ocean   ocean

office

[ɔ́:fis] 오피스

사무실

office office office office

old

[ould] 오울드

늙은, 오래된

old old old old old

on

[ən] 언

~ 위에

on on on on on on

out

[aut] 아웃

~ 밖에

out out out out out

part

[pɑ:rt] 파−트

부분, 일부

part part part part

pass

[pæs] 패스

통과하다

pass　pass　pass　pass

peach

[pi:tʃ] 피-취

복숭아

peach　peach　peach　peach

people

[pí:pl] 피-플

사람들

people　people　people

person

[pə́:rsn] 퍼-슨

사람

person　person　person　person

pet

[pet] 펟

애완동물

pet　pet　pet　pet　pet

picnic
[píknik] 피크닉

소풍

picnic   picnic   picnic   picnic

picture
[píktʃər] 픽쳐

그림, 사진

picture   picture   picture

pie
[pai] 파이

파이

pie   pie   pie   pie   pie

pink
[piŋk] 핑크

분홍색

pink   pink   pink   pink

plant
[plænt] 플랜트

식물

plant   plant   plant   plant

post
[poust] 포우스트
우편

post   post   post   post

post office
[póust ɔːfis] 포우스트 오피스
우체국

post office   post office

price
[prais] 프라이스
값, 가격

price   price   price   price

puppy
[pʌ́pi] 퍼피
강아지

puppy   puppy   puppy

put
[put] 풋
두다, 놓다

put   put   put   put   put

rainy
[réini] 레이니

비가 오는

rainy   rainy   rainy   rainy

read
[ri:d] 리-드

읽다

read   read   read   read

red
[red] 레드

빨간색

red   red   red   red   red

rest
[rest] 레스트

휴식

rest   rest   rest   rest   rest

restroom
[restrum] 레스트룸

화장실

restroom   restroom

ribbon

[ríbən] 리번

리본

ribbon ribbon ribbon ribbon

rich

[ritʃ] 리취

부유한

rich rich rich rich rich

right

[rait] 라이트

옳은

right right right right

rock

[rɑk] 락

바위

rock rock rock rock

roof

[ruːf] 루-프

지붕

roof roof roof roof

run

[rʌn] 런

달리다

run   run   run   run   run

salad

[sǽləd] 샐러드

샐러드

salad   salad   salad   salad

sand

[sænd] 샌드

모래

sand   sand   sand   sand

see

[siː] 씨-

보다

see   see   see   see   see

she

[ʃiː] 쉬-

그녀

she   she   she   she   she

sheep
[ʃi:p] 쉬-ㅍ
양

sheep sheep sheep sheep

shopping
[ʃápiŋ] 샤핑
쇼핑

shopping shopping shopping

short
[ʃɔ:rt] 쇼-트
짧은

short short short short

sick
[sik] 식
아픈

sick sick sick sick sick

silver
[sílvər] 실버
은, 은색의

silver silver silver silver

sit
[sit] 씨트

앉다

sit   sit   sit   sit   sit   sit

skirt
[skə:rt] 스커-트

치마

skirt   skirt   skirt   skirt

snake
[sneik] 스네이크

뱀

snake   snake   snake   snake

soap
[soup] 쏘웁

비누

soap   soap   soap   soap

soccer
[sákər] 싸커

축구

soccer   soccer   soccer   soccer

sock
[sɑk] 싹

양말

sock   sock   sock   sock

sofa
[sóufə] 쏘우퍼

소파

sofa   sofa   sofa   sofa

sound
[saund] 싸운드

소리

sound   sound   sound   sound

soup
[su:p] 쑤-프

수프

soup   soup   soup   soup

south
[sauθ] 싸우쓰

남쪽

south   south   south   south

space
[speis] 스페이스

공간, 우주

space   space   space   space

spoon
[spu:n] 스푸ーㄴ

숟가락

spoon   spoon   spoon   spoon

sport
[spɔ:rt] 스포ー트

스포츠

sport   sport   sport   sport

stamp
[stæmp] 스탬프

도장

stamp   stamp   stamp   stamp

stand
[stænd] 스탠드

서다

stand   stand   stand   stand

start

[stɑːrt] 스타-트

시작하다

start start start start

stone

[stoun] 스토운

돌

stone stone stone stone

strong

[strɔːŋ] 스트로-ㅇ

강한, 힘센

strong strong strong strong

study

[stʌ́di] 스터디

공부하다

study study study study

style

[stail] 스타일

스타일, 방식

style style style style

sunny
[sʌ́ni] 써니

맑은, 화창한

sunny sunny sunny sunny

sure
[ʃuər] 슈어

물론

sure   sure   sure   sure

sweater
[swétər] 스웨터

스웨터

sweater   sweater   sweater

tail
[teil] 테일

꼬리

tail   tail   tail   tail   tail

tape
[teip] 테이프

테이프

tape   tape   tape   tape

team
[ti:m] 티-ㅁ
팀, 단체

team team team team

tell
[tel] 텔
말하다

tell tell tell tell tell

tent
[tent] 텐트
텐트

tent tent tent tent

test
[test] 테스트
시험

test test test test

there
[ðέər] 데어
거기에

there there there there

ticket
[tíkit] 티킽

표, 티켓

ticket ticket ticket ticket

tiger
[táigər] 타이거

호랑이

tiger tiger tiger tiger

tired
[taiərd] 타이어드

피곤한

tired tired tired tired

toilet
[tɔ́ilit] 토일맅

화장실, 변기

toilet toilet toilet toilet

tonight
[tənáit] 터나잍

오늘밤

tonight tonight tonight

top
[tɑp] 탑

꼭대기, 정상

top top top top top

touch
[tʌtʃ] 터취

만지다

touch touch touch touch

town
[taun] 타운

마을, 동네

town town town town

traffic
[træfik] 트래픽

교통

traffic traffic traffic traffic

travel
[trævl] 트래블

여행하다, 여행

travel travel travel travel

uncle
[ʌ́ŋkl] 엉클
삼촌

uncle   uncle   uncle   uncle

vacation
[veikéiʃən] 베이케이션
방학, 휴가

vacation   vacation   vacation

very
[véri] 베리
매우, 대단히

very   very   very   very

view
[vjuː] 뷰-
경치, 전망

view   view   view   view

walk
[wɔːk] 워-크
걷다

walk   walk   walk   walk

want
[wɔ:nt] 원트

원하다

want　want　want　want

weather
[wéðər] 웨더

날씨

weather　weather　weather

west
[west] 웨스트

서쪽

west　west　west　west

white
[hwait] 와이트

흰색

white　white　white　white

win
[win] 윈

이기다

win　win　win　win　win

windy

[wíndi] 윈디

바람 부는

windy   windy   windy   windy

wing

[wiŋ] 윙

날개

wing   wing   wing   wing

woman

[wúmən] 우먼

(성인) 여자

woman   woman   woman

x-ray

[éksrèi] 엑스레이

엑스레이

x-ray   x-ray   x-ray   x-ray

yellow

[jélou] 옐로우

노란색

yellow   yellow   yellow

재미있는 영단어 퀴즈

1 아래 그림을 보고 빈칸을 채워 영단어를 완성하세요.

1) br＿＿＿＿   2) ch＿＿ch   3) ear＿＿

4) sh＿＿p   5) ＿＿＿dle   6) lett＿＿

2 아래 보기에서 알맞은 우리말을 찾아 쓰세요.

> **보기**
>
> 초록색 꿈 암탉 그림 쉬운 직업

1) easy ＿＿＿＿   4) job ＿＿＿＿

2) green ＿＿＿＿   5) picture ＿＿＿＿

3) dream ＿＿＿＿   6) hen ＿＿＿＿

112

3 우리말에 맞게 영단어를 바르게 써 보세요.

> **보기**
>
> i g t r e ➡ 호랑이 _tiger_

1) d o o f
음식 _____

4) r t o s p
스포츠 _____

2) d i r n k
마시다 _____

5) f x o
여우 _____

3) n u r e s
간호사 _____

6) m a k e r t
시장 _____

4 영단어에 알맞은 우리말을 줄로 연결하세요.

1) mouse ·   · 기린
2) heart ·   · 쥐
3) kitchen ·   · 주방
4) giraffe ·   · 심장

5 우리말에 알맞은 영단어를 쓰고 퍼즐을 완성하세요.

bedroom   eat   morning
soccer   classroom   dance

교실

춤추다

침실

먹다   a

축구   d

c

o   아침

5. 교실 classroom / 먹다 eat / 아침 morning / 춤추다 dance / 침실 bedroom / 축구 soccer

114

5학년
필수 영단어
따라쓰기

able

[éibl] 에이블

~할 수 있는

able able able able

about

[əbáut] 어바웉

~에 대한

about about about about

act

[ækt] 액트

행동하다

act act act act act

action

[ǽkʃən] 액션

행동

action action action action

actor

[ǽktər] 액터

배우

actor actor actor actor

actress
[ǽktris] 액트리스

여배우

actress actress actress actress

address
[ədrés] 어드레스

주소

address address address

after
[ǽftər] 앱터

~ 뒤에, ~ 후에

after after after after

again
[əgén] 어겐

다시

again again again again

ago
[əgóu] 어고우

~ 전에

ago ago ago ago ago

ahead
[əhéd] 어헤드
앞에, 앞으로

ahead   ahead   ahead

alone
[əlóun] 얼로운
혼자

alone   alone   alone   alone

alphabet
[ǽlfəbèt] 앨퍼벹
알파벳

alphabet   alphabet   alphabet

also
[ɔ́:lsou] 오-ㄹ소우
또한, 역시

also   also   also   also   also

and
[ænd] 앤드
그리고, ~와

and   and   and   and   and

answer
[ǽnsər] 앤서
대답, 답하다

answer   answer   answer

arrive
[əráiv] 어라이브
도착하다

arrive   arrive   arrive   arrive

ask
[æsk] 애스크
묻다

ask   ask   ask   ask   ask

?

at
[æt] 앹
~에

at   at   at   at   at   at

attend
[əténd] 어텐드
출석하다

attend   attend   attend

aunt
[ænt] 앤트

이모, 고모

aunt   aunt   aunt   aunt

autumn
[ɔ́:təm] 오-텀

가을

autumn   autumn   autumn

backyard
[bǽkjɑ́:rd] 백야-드

뒤뜰

backyard   backyard   backyard

before
[bifɔ́:r] 비포-

~ 전에

before   before   before

begin
[bigín] 비긴

시작하다

begin   begin   begin   begin

behind
[biháind] 비하인드
~ 뒤에

behind   behind   behind

best
[best] 베스트
최고의

best   best   best   best

bicycle
[báisikəl] 바이시컬
자전거

bicycle   bicycle   bicycle

blackboard
[blǽkbòːrd] 블랙보−드
칠판

blackboard   blackboard

blanket
[blǽŋkit] 블랭킽
이불

blanket   blanket   blanket

blood
[blʌd] 블러드

피, 혈액

blood   blood   blood

bookstore
[búkstɔ̀ːr] 북스토-

서점

bookstore   bookstore

build
[bild] 빌드

짓다, 세우다

build   build   build   build

but
[bʌt] 벗

그러나

but   but   but   but   but

by
[bai] 바이

~ 옆에

by   by   by   by   by   by

calendar
[kǽlindər] 캘린더

달력

calendar   calendar   calendar

captain
[kǽptin] 캡틴

선장, 장

captain   captain   captain

catch
[kætʃ] 캐취

잡다

catch   catch   catch   catch

cave
[keiv] 케이브

동굴

cave   cave   cave   cave

center
[séntər] 센터

중심, 중앙

center   center   center   center

chance
[tʃæns] 챈스

기회, 가능성

chance   chance   chance

check
[tʃek] 체크

확인하다

check   check   check   check

choose
[tʃuːz] 츄-즈

선택하다

choose   choose   choose

circle
[sə́ːrkl] 서-클

원, 동그라미

circle   circle   circle   circle

clear
[kliər] 클리어

맑은

clear   clear   clear   clear

clever

[klévər] 클레버

영리한

clever clever clever clever

cloth

[klɔ:θ] 클로쓰

천

cloth cloth cloth cloth

clothes

[klouz] 클로우즈

옷, 의상

clothes clothes clothes

company

[kʌ́mpəni] 컴퍼니

회사

company company

condition

[kəndíʃən] 컨디션

상태, 조건

condition condition condition

country

[kʌ́ntri] 컨트리

나라, 국가

country   country   country

cover

[kʌ́vər] 커버

덮다, 씌우다

cover   cover   cover   cover

curtain

[kə́ːrtn] 커-튼

커튼

curtain   curtain   curtain

dear

[diər] 디어

사랑하는, 소중한

dear   dear   dear   dear

deep

[diːp] 디-프

깊은, 짙은

deep   deep   deep   deep

dirty
[də́:rti] 더-티

더러운

dirty dirty dirty dirty

dollar
[dálər] 달러

달러

dollar dollar dollar dollar

dolphin
[dálfin] 달핀

돌고래

dolphin dolphin dolphin

drop
[drɑp] 드랍

떨어지다

drop drop drop drop

early
[ə́:rli] 어-리

일찍, 이른

early early early early

elevator
[éləvèitər] 엘리베이터

엘리베이터

elevator elevator elevator

empty
[émpti] 엠프티

비어 있는

empty empty empty empty

enter
[éntər] 엔터

~에 들어가다

enter enter enter enter

excuse
[ikskjúːz] 익스큐-즈

용서하다

excuse excuse excuse excuse

fan
[fæn] 팬

선풍기

fan fan fan fan fan

fast

[fæst] 패스트

빠른

fast fast fast fast

feed

[fi:d] 피―드

먹이, 먹이를 주다

feed feed feed feed

feel

[fi:l] 피―ㄹ

느끼다

feel feel feel feel

find

[faind] 파인드

찾다

find find find find

fine

[fain] 파인

좋은

fine fine fine fine

finger

[fíŋgər] 핑거

손가락

finger finger finger finger

flag

[flæg] 플래그

깃발, 기

flag flag flag flag flag

floor

[flɔ:r] 플로-

바닥, 층

floor floor floor floor

fool

[fu:l] 푸울

바보

fool fool fool fool

foolish

[fú:liʃ] 풀-리쉬

바보 같은

foolish foolish foolish

forest
[fɔ́ːrist] 포리스트
숲

forest forest forest forest

fresh
[freʃ] 프레쉬
신선한

fresh fresh fresh fresh

from
[frʌm] 프럼
~부터

from from from from

full
[ful] 풀
가득 찬

full full full full full

future
[fjúːtʃər] 퓨-쳐
미래

future future future

get
[get] 겟
얻다

get   get   get   get   get

give
[giv] 기브
주다

give   give   give   give

glove
[glʌv] 글러브
장갑

glove   glove   glove   glove

goat
[gout] 고우트
염소

goat   goat   goat   goat

granddaughter
[grǽnddɔ̀:tər] 그랜도-터
손녀

granddaughter   granddaughter

grandfather
[grǽndfɑ̀ːðər] 그랜파-더

할아버지

grandfather   grandfather

grandmother
[grǽndmʌ̀ðər] 그랜머더

할머니

grandmother   grandmother

grandson
[grǽndsʌ́n] 그랜썬

손자

grandson   grandson   grandson

grass
[grǽs] 그래스

잔디, 풀

grass   grass   grass   grass

ground
[graund] 그라운드

지면, 땅

ground   ground   ground

guitar

[gitá:r] 기타-

기타

guitar guitar guitar guitar

hamburger

[hǽmbə̀:rgər] 햄버-거

햄버거

hamburger hamburger

head

[hed] 헤드

머리

head   head   head   head

headache

[hédèik] 헤데익

두통

headache   headache

health

[helθ] 헬쓰

건강

health   health   health

hit
[hit] 힡

치다, 때리다

hit hit hit hit hit

hobby
[hábi] 하비

취미

hobby hobby hobby hobby

holiday
[hálǝdèi] 할러데이

휴일, 휴가

holiday holiday holiday

how
[hau] 하우

어떻게

how how how how how

ill
[il] 일

아픈

ill ill ill ill ill ill

jeans
[dʒiːnz] 진-즈

청바지

jeans jeans jeans jeans

join
[dʒɔin] 조인

참여하다, 가입하다

join join join join join

joy
[dʒɔi] 죠이

기쁨, 즐거움

joy joy joy joy joy

jungle
[dʒʌ́ŋgl] 정글

정글, 밀림

jungle jungle jungle

just
[dʒʌst] 저스트

막

just just just just just

kangaroo
[kǽŋgərúː] 캥거루-

캥거루

kangaroo   kangaroo   kangaroo

kick
[kik] 킥

차다, 킥

kick   kick   kick   kick   kick

kitty
[kíti] 키티

새끼 고양이

kitty   kitty   kitty   kitty

knife
[naif] 나이프

칼

knife   knife   knife   knife

knock
[nɑk] 낙

두드리다

knock   knock   knock

lead
[li:d] 리-드
이끌다

lead　lead　lead　lead

leader
[líːdər] 리더
지도자

leader　leader　leader

leaf
[liːf] 리-프
나뭇잎

leaf　leaf　leaf　leaf

learn
[ləːrn] 런-
배우다

learn　learn　learn　learn

leave
[liːv] 리-브
떠나다

leave　leave　leave　leave

left
[left] 레프트

왼쪽

left　left　left　left　left

lesson
[lésn] 레슨

수업, 연습

lesson　lesson　lesson　lesson

lie
[lai] 라이

거짓말, 눕다

lie　lie　lie　lie　lie　lie

life
[laif] 라이프

인생, 삶

life　life　life　life　life

listen
[lísn] 리슨

듣다

listen　listen　listen　listen

little
[lítl] 리틀
작은

little little little little

live
[liv] 리브
살다

live live live live live

lock
[lak] 락
잠그다

lock lock lock lock

math
[mæθ] 매스
수학

math math math math

2+3=5

middle
[mídl] 미들
중앙, 가운데

middle middle middle

mind
[maind] 마인드
마음

mind   mind   mind   mind

miss
[mis] 미스
놓치다

miss   miss   miss   miss

mistake
[mistéik] 미스테익
실수

mistake   mistake   mistake

mix
[miks] 믹스
섞다

mix   mix   mix   mix   mix

model
[mádl] 마들
모델, 모형

model   model   model   model

more
[mɔːr] 모-
좀 더

more　more　more　more

mountain
[máuntən] 마운턴
산

mountain　mountain　mountain

museum
[mjuːzíːəm] 뮤-지엄
박물관

museum　museum　museum

musical
[mjúːzikəl] 뮤-지컬
뮤지컬

musical　musical　musical

musician
[mjuːzíʃən] 뮤-지션
음악가

musician　musician　musician

must
[mʌst] 머스트
~해야 한다

must must must must

nest
[nest] 네스트
둥지

nest nest nest nest

night
[nait] 나이트
밤

night night night night

of
[ʌv] 업
~의

of of of of of of

once
[wʌns] 원스
한 번

once once once once

only [óunli] 오운리 유일한, 단 하나의	only only only only
oops [ups] 웁스 (감탄사) 이크, 이런	oops oops oops oops
outside [àutsáid] 아웃사이드 밖	outside outside outside
over [óuvər] 오우버 ~ 위에	over over over over
page [peidʒ] 페이쥐 페이지, 쪽	page page page page

parent
[pέərənt] 페어런트
부모

parent   parent   parent

perfect
[pə́:rfikt] 퍼-픽트
완벽한

perfect   perfect   perfect

pick
[pik] 픽
고르다

pick   pick   pick   pick

piece
[pi:s] 피-스
조각

piece   piece   piece   piece

pineapple
[páinæ̀pl] 파인애플
파인애플

pineapple   pineapple

place
[pleis] 플레이스

장소

place place place place

plan
[plæn] 플랜

계획, 계획하다

plan plan plan plan

plus
[plʌs] 플러스

더하기, 더하다

plus plus plus plus

pocket
[pάkit] 파킫

주머니

pocket pocket pocket

pool
[puːl] 푸-울

수영장, 풀

pool pool pool pool

poster

[póustər] 포우스터

포스터

poster poster poster poster

pot

[pɑt] 팓

냄비

pot pot pot pot pot

power

[páuər] 파워

권력, 힘

power power power

present

[préznt] 프레즌트

선물

present present present

press

[pres] 프레스

누르다

press press press press

print
[print] 프린트

인쇄하다

print print print print

problem
[prábləm] 프라블럼

문제

problem problem problem

pull
[pul] 풀

끌다, 당기다

pull pull pull pull pull

pure
[pjuər] 퓨어

순수한

pure pure pure pure

purple
[pə́:rpl] 퍼―플

보라색

purple purple purple

push
[puʃ] 푸쉬
밀다

push   push   push   push

race
[reis] 레이스
경주, 경기

race   race   race   race

ready
[rédi] 레디
준비된

ready   ready   ready   ready

real
[ríːəl] 리-얼
진짜의, 진실의

real   real   real   real

really
[ríːəli] 리-얼리
정말로

really   really   really   really

restaurant
[réstərənt] 레스터런트
식당

restaurant   restaurant   restaurant

review
[rivjú:] 리뷰-
복습하다

review   review   review

sad
[sæd] 새드
슬픈

sad   sad   sad   sad   sad

safe
[seif] 세이프
안전한

safe   safe   safe   safe

save
[seiv] 세이브
저축하다, 절약하다

save   save   save   save

say
[sei] 세이

말하다

say   say   say   say   say

science
[sáiəns] 사이언스

과학

science   science   science

scientist
[sáiəntist] 사이언티스트

과학자

scientist   scientist   scientist

score
[skɔːr] 스코-

점수

score   score   score   score

seat
[siːt] 씨-트

자리, 좌석

seat   seat   seat   seat

sell
[sel] 셀
팔다

sell sell sell sell sell

send
[send] 센드
보내다

send send send send

service
[sə́:rvis] 서-비스
서비스, 봉사

service service service

set
[set] 셑
놓다, 두다

set set set set set

show
[ʃou] 쇼우
보여주다

show show show show

sign
[sain] 사인

간판, 서명하다

sign   sign   sign   sign

simple
[símpl] 심플

간단한

simple   simple   simple

sir
[səːr] 써-

~씨, ~님

sir   sir   sir   sir   sir

size
[saiz] 싸이즈

크기, 치수

size   size   size   size

sleep
[sliːp] 슬리-ㅍ

자다

sleep   sleep   sleep   sleep

slow
[slou] 슬로우

느린

slow slow slow slow

smell
[smel] 스멜

냄새가 나다

smell smell smell smell

soft
[sɔːft] 소프트

부드러운

soft soft soft soft

some
[sʌm] 썸

일부, 약간의

some some some some

speak
[spiːk] 스피-크

말하다

speak speak speak speak

speech
[spi:tʃ] 스피-취

연설

speech   speech   speech

speed
[spi:d] 스피-드

속도

speed   speed   speed   speed

spring
[spriŋ] 스프링

봄

spring   spring   spring   spring

stair
[stɛər] 스테어

계단

stair   stair   stair   stair

station
[stéiʃən] 스테이션

역

station   station   station

stay
[stei] 스테이

머물다

stay   stay   stay   stay

step
[step] 스텝

걸음, 단계

step   step   step   step

strawberry
[strɔ́ːbèri] 스트로-베리

딸기

strawberry   strawberry

street
[striːt] 스트리-트

거리, 도로

street   street   street   street

subway
[sʌ́bwèi] 섭웨이

지하철

subway   subway   subway

summer
[sʌ́mər] 써머
여름

summer summer summer

take
[teik] 테이크
잡다

take take take take

talk
[tɔːk] 토-크
말하다

talk talk talk talk

tall
[tɔːl] 토-ㄹ
키가 큰

tall tall tall tall

telephone
[téləfòun] 텔러포운
전화

telephone telephone

tennis
[ténis] 테니스
테니스

tennis tennis tennis tennis

think
[θiŋk] 씽크
생각하다

think think think think

tie
[tai] 타이
넥타이, 묶다

tie tie tie tie tie tie

to
[tuː] 투-
~로, ~쪽으로

to to to to to to

today
[tədéi] 터데이
오늘

today today today today

toe
[tou] 토우

발가락

toe   toe   toe   toe   toe

together
[təgéðər] 터게더

함께

together   together   together

tomorrow
[təmɔ́ːrou] 터모-로우

내일

tomorrow   tomorrow   tomorrow

towel
[táuəl] 타월

수건

towel   towel   towel   towel

try
[trai] 트라이

노력하다

try   try   try   try   try   try

turn
[təːrn] 터-언
돌다

turn　turn　turn　turn

under
[ʌ́ndər] 언더
~ 아래에

under under under under

uniform
[júːnifɔ̀ːrm] 유-니폼-
제복, 유니폼

uniform　uniform　uniform

use
[juːs] 유-스
사용하다

use　use　use　use　use

vegetable
[védʒətəbl] 베쥐터블
채소

vegetable vegetable vegetable

village

[vílidʒ] 빌리쥐

마을

village village village village

visit

[vízit] 비짙

방문하다

visit   visit   visit   visit

voice

[vɔis] 보이스

목소리

voice   voice   voice   voice

wake

[weik] 웨이크

(잠에서) 깨다

wake   wake   wake   wake

wave

[weiv] 웨이브

파도

wave   wave   wave   wave

way
[wei] 웨이
길, 방법

way way way way way

we
[wi:] 위-
우리

we we we we we we

wear
[wɛər] 웨어
입다

wear wear wear wear

well
[wel] 웰
잘, 좋게

well well well well

wet
[wet] 웹
젖은, 축축한

wet wet wet wet wet

what

[hwɑt] 왙

무엇

what what what what

when

[hwen] 웬

언제

when when when when

where

[hwɛər] 웨어

어디

where where where where

who

[huː] 후

누구

who who who who who

why

[hwai] 와이

왜

why why why why why

wide
[waid] 와이드
넓은

wide　wide　wide　wide

wife
[waif] 와이프
아내, 부인

wife　wife　wife　wife

winter
[wíntər] 윈터
겨울

winter　winter　winter　winter

wish
[wiʃ] 위쉬
원하다

wish　wish　wish　wish

with
[wið] 위드
~와 함께

with　with　with　with

wonderful

[wʌ́ndərfəl] 원더펄

훌륭한

wonderful wonderful wonderful

write

[rait] 라이트

쓰다

write write write write

wrong

[rɔ́ːŋ] 롱-

틀린, 잘못된

wrong wrong wrong wrong

yesterday

[jéstərdèi] 예스터데이

어제

yesterday yesterday yesterday

young

[jʌŋ] 영

어린, 젊은

young young young

재미있는 **영단어 퀴즈**

1 아래 그림을 보고 빈칸을 채워 영단어를 완성하세요.

1) _ _ _phin

2) ni_ _ _t

3) glo_ _ _

4) _ _ _burger

5) ten_ _ _ _

6) p_ t

2 아래 보기에서 알맞은 우리말을 찾아 쓰세요.

> **보기**
>
> 자전거 일찍 나뭇잎 듣다 나라 행동

1) listen _____

2) action _____

3) early _____

4) country _____

5) bicycle _____

6) leaf _____

우리말에 맞게 영단어를 바르게 써 보세요.

보기

b b h o y ➡ 취미 <u>hobby</u>

1) h a e d
머리 _____

4) f t l e
왼쪽 _____

2) a g f l
깃발 _____

5) s d a
슬픈 _____

3) a c e v
동굴 _____

6) i n w t r e
겨울 _____

4 영단어에 알맞은 우리말을 줄로 연결하세요.

1) future ·   · 부모

2) address ·   · 대답

3) parent ·   · 미래

4) answer ·   · 주소

 정 답

4. 1) future 미래 2) address 주소 3) parent 부모 4) answer 대답

3. 1) head 머리 2) flag 깃발 3) cave 동굴 4) left 왼쪽 5) sad 슬픈 6) winter 겨울

5 우리말에 알맞은 영단어를 쓰고 퍼즐을 완성하세요.

today   holiday   ask
bookstore   race   little

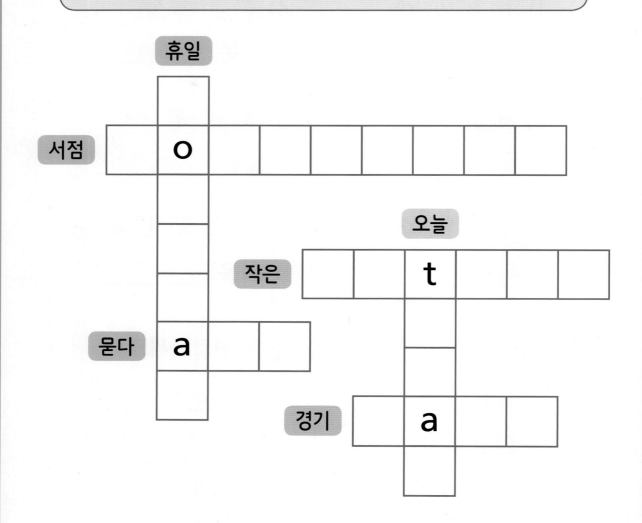

휴일

서점   o

오늘

작은   t

묻다   a

경기   a

5. 휴일 holiday / 서점 bookstore / 묻다 ask / 오늘 today / 작은 little / 경기 race

6학년

필수 영단어
따라쓰기

absent
[ǽbsənt] 앱선트
결석한

absent absent absent absent

accident
[ǽksidənt] 액시던트
사고

accident accident accident

advice
[ədváis] 어드바이스
충고, 조언

advice advice advice

agree
[əgríː] 어그리－
동의하다

agree agree agree agree

Yes

allow
[əláu] 얼라우
허락하다

allow allow allow allow

almost

[ɔ́ːlmoust] 올-모우스트

거의

almost almost almost almost

already

[ɔːlrédi] 오-ㄹ레디

이미

already already already

always

[ɔ́ːlweiz] 오-ㄹ웨이즈

항상

always always always

another

[ənʌ́ðər] 어너더

또 하나의

another another another

any

[éni] 에니

어떤, 어느

any any any any any

anything
[éniθiŋ] 에니씽

무엇이든, 아무것도

anything anything anything

anyway
[éniwèi] 에니웨이

어쨌든

anyway anyway anyway

around
[əráund] 어라운드

주위에

around around around

away
[əwéi] 어웨이

떨어져

away away away away

badminton
[bǽdmintən] 배드민턴

배드민턴

badminton badminton

baseball
[béisbɔ̀:l] 베이스보-ㄹ
야구

baseball   baseball   baseball

basketball
[bǽskitbɔ̀:l] 베스킽보-ㄹ
농구

basketball   basketball   basketball

because
[bikɔ́:z] 비코-즈
～때문에, 왜냐하면

because   because   because

become
[bikʌ́m] 비컴
～이 되다

become   become   become

believe
[bilí:v] 빌리-브
믿다

believe   believe   believe

bench
[bentʃ] 벤취
벤치, 긴 의자

bench bench bench bench

better
[bétər] 베터
더 좋은

better better better better

between
[bitwíːn] 비트위ㅡㄴ
~사이에

between between between

blossom
[blásəm] 블라섬
꽃, 꽃피다

blossom blossom blossom

both
[bouθ] 보우쓰
둘 다

both both both both

bottom
[bátəm] 바텀

밑, 밑바닥

bottom   bottom   bottom

break
[breik] 브레이크

깨다, 부수다

break   break   break   break

bright
[brait] 브라이트

밝은

bright   bright   bright   bright

bring
[briŋ] 브링

가져오다, 데려오다

bring   bring   bring   bring

broad
[brɔ:d] 브로-드

넓은

broad   broad   broad   broad

brush
[brʌʃ] 브러시

빗, 솔, 빗질하다

brush brush brush brush

bucket
[bʌ́kit] 버킽

양동이

bucket bucket bucket

building
[bíldiŋ] 빌딩

건물

building building building

careful
[kέərfəl] 케어펄

조심스러운, 주의 깊은

careful careful careful

carry
[kǽri] 캐리

나르다

carry carry carry carry

ceiling
[síːliŋ] 시-일링

천장

ceiling ceiling ceiling ceiling

change
[tʃeindʒ] 체인쥐

변하다, 바꾸다

change change change

cheap
[tʃiːp] 치-프

(값이) 싼

cheap cheap cheap cheap

cheek
[tʃiːk] 치-크

볼, 뺨

cheek cheek cheek cheek

chopstick
[tʃápstik] 찹스틱

젓가락

chopstick chopstick chopstick

collect
[kəlékt] 컬렉트
모으다

collect collect collect collect

cone
[koun] 코운
원뿔

cone cone cone cone

congratulate
[kəngrǽtʃulèit] 컨그래춰레이트
축하하다

congratulate congratulate

continue
[kəntínju:] 컨티뉴-
계속하다

continue continue continue

corner
[kɔ́:rnər] 코-너
구석, 모퉁이

corner corner corner corner

correct

[kərékt] 커렉트

정확한

correct correct correct correct

cost

[kɔ:st] 코-스트

비용, 대가

cost cost cost cost

count

[kaunt] 카운트

세다, 계산하다

count count count count

course

[kɔ:rs] 코-스

코스, 과정

course course course course

cousin

[kʌzn] 커즌

사촌

cousin cousin cousin cousin

danger

[déindʒər] 데인저

위험

danger danger danger danger

daughter

[dɔ́ːtər] 도-터

딸

daughter daughter daughter

delicious

[dilíʃəs] 딜리셔스

맛있는

delicious delicious delicious

dictionary

[díkʃənèri] 딕셔너리

사전

dictionary dictionary dictionary

different

[dífərənt] 디퍼런트

다른

different different different

difficult
[dífikʌlt] 디피컬트
어려운

difficult difficult difficult

earache
[íərèik] 이어레익
귀앓이

earache earache earache

elementary
[èləméntəri] 엘러멘터리
기초의, 초등의

elementary elementary

1+2=3

enough
[inʌf] 이너프
충분한

enough enough enough

every
[évri] 에브리
모든

every every every every

everywhere

[évriwɛ̀ər] 에브리웨어

어디나, 모든 곳

everywhere   everywhere

example

[igzǽmpl] 익잼플

예

example   example   example

excellent

[éksələnt] 엑설런트

훌륭한

excellent   excellent   excellent

excite

[iksáit] 익사이트

흥분시키다

excite   excite   excite   excite

exciting

[iksáitiŋ] 익사이팅

신나는, 흥미진진한

exciting   exciting   exciting

expensive

[ikspénsiv] 익스펜시브

비싼

expensive   expensive

factory

[fæktəri] 팩터리

공장

factory   factory   factory

fall

[fɔ:l] 포-ㄹ

떨어지다

fall   fall   fall   fall   fall

far

[fɑ:r] 파-

멀리

far   far   far   far   far

favorite

[féivərit] 페이버릳

매우 좋아하는

favorite   favorite   favorite

few
[fju:] 퓨-

(수가) 적은

few few few few

field
[fi:ld] 필-드

들판, 밭

field field field field

fight
[fait] 파이트

싸우다

fight fight fight fight

fill
[fil] 필

채우다

fill fill fill fill fill

finish
[fíniʃ] 피니쉬

끝내다, 마치다

finish finish finish finish

fix
[fiks] 픽스
고치다, 고정하다

fix   fix   fix   fix   fix

fog
[fɔːg] 포그
안개

fog   fog   fog   fog   fog

foggy
[fɔ́ːgi] 포-기
안개가 낀

foggy   foggy   foggy   foggy

follow
[fɑ́lou] 팔로우
따르다, 뒤를 잇다

follow   follow   follow   follow

forget
[fərgét] 퍼겓
잊다

forget   forget   forget   forget

front
[frʌnt] 프런트

앞, 정면

front   front   front   front

gather
[gǽðər] 개더

모이다

gather gather gather gather

gentle
[dʒéntl] 젠틀

순한, 온화한

gentle gentle gentle gentle

gentleman
[dʒéntlmən] 젠틀먼

신사

gentleman   gentleman

glad
[glæd] 글래드

기쁜

glad   glad   glad   glad

glue
[glu:] 글루-

풀

glue glue glue glue

grow
[grou] 그로우

자라다

grow grow grow grow

guess
[ges] 게스

추측하다

guess guess guess guess

guide
[gaid] 가이드

길잡이, 안내자

guide guide guide guide

habit
[hǽbit] 해빝

버릇, 습관

habit habit habit habit

half
[hæf] 해프

반, 절반

half half half half

handsome
[hǽnsəm] 핸섬

멋진, 잘생긴

handsome handsome

hang
[hæŋ] 행

걸다, 매달리다

hang hang hang hang

hard
[hɑːrd] 하―드

딱딱한, 어려운

hard hard hard hard

harvest
[hɑ́ːrvist] 하―비스트

추수하다

harvest harvest harvest

hate
[heit] 헤잍

미워하다

hate   hate   hate   hate

heavy
[hévi] 헤비

무거운

heavy   heavy   heavy   heavy

helicopter
[hélikàptər] 헬리캅터

헬리콥터

helicopter   helicopter

hide
[haid] 하이드

숨기다, 감추다

hide   hide   hide   hide

hiking
[háikiŋ] 하이킹

하이킹, 보도 여행

hiking   hiking   hiking   hiking

history
[hístəri] 히스터리
역사

history　history　history

hold
[hould] 호울드
잡다, 쥐다

hold　hold　hold　hold

hole
[houl] 호울
구멍

hole　hole　hole　hole

honest
[ánist] 아니스트
정직한

honest honest honest honest

honey
[hʌni] 허니
꿀, 여보

honey　honey　honey　honey

hope
[houp] 호웁

바라다

hope　hope　hope　hope

hurt
[həːrt] 허-트

다친, 아프다

hurt　hurt　hurt　hurt

husband
[hʌ́zbənd] 허즈번드

남편

husband　husband　husband

if
[if] 이프

만약 ~라면

if　if　if　if　if　if

important
[impɔ́ːrtənt] 임포-턴트

중요한

important　important　important

insect
[ínsekt] 인섹트
곤충

insect insect insect insect

inside
[ìnsáid] 인사이드
안쪽, 내부

inside inside inside inside

interesting
[íntəristiŋ] 인터리스팅
재미있는, 흥미로운

interesting interesting

into
[íntu] 인투
~ 안으로

into into into into

introduce
[ìntrədjúːs] 인트러듀-스
소개하다

introduce introduce introduce

invite
[inváit] 인바이트
초대하다

invite invite invite invite

island
[áilənd] 아일런드
섬

island island island island

keep
[ki:p] 킵-
계속하다

keep keep keep keep

lamb
[læm] 램
어린 양

lamb lamb lamb lamb

language
[læŋgwidʒ] 랭귀쥐
언어

language language language

large
[lɑ:rdʒ] 라-쥐
넓은

large large large large

last
[læst] 래스트
지난

last last last last

laugh
[læf] 래프
웃다

laugh laugh laugh laugh

laundry
[lɔ́:ndri] 론드리
세탁물, 세탁

laundry laundry laundry

law
[lɔ:] 로-
법

law law law law law

lazy
[léizi] 레이지
게으른

lazy   lazy   lazy   lazy

lend
[lend] 렌드
빌려주다

lend   lend   lend   lend

level
[lévl] 레블
레벨, 수준

level   level   level   level

lift
[lift] 리프트
올리다, 승강기

lift   lift   lift   lift   lift

light
[lait] 라이트
빛, 가벼운

light   light   light   light

lonely
[lóunli] 로운리

외로운

lonely   lonely   lonely

lose
[lu:z] 루－즈

잃다, 지다

lose   lose   lose   lose

loss
[lɔ:s] 로스

잃음, 손해

loss   loss   loss   loss

loud
[laud] 라우드

시끄러운

loud   loud   loud   loud

lucky
[lʌ́ki] 러키

운이 좋은

lucky   lucky   lucky   lucky

machine
[məʃíːn] 머쉬-인

기계

machine machine machine

magazine
[mǽgəziːn] 매거지-ㄴ

잡지

magazine magazine magazine

match
[mætʃ] 매취

경기, 시합

match match match match

matter
[mǽtər] 매터

문제, 일

matter matter matter matter

may
[mei] 메이

~일지도 모른다

may may may may

meal
[mi:l] 미-ㄹ

식사

meal meal meal meal

mean
[mi:n] 미-ㄴ

의미하다

mean mean mean mean

melon
[mélən] 멜런

멜론

melon melon melon melon

most
[moust] 모우스트

대부분

most most most most

move
[mu:v] 무-브

움직이다

move move move move

narrow
[nǽrou] 내로우
좁은

narrow narrow narrow

nation
[néiʃən] 네이션
국가, 국민

nation nation nation

near
[niər] 니어
근처, 가까운

near near near near

necklace
[néklis] 넥클리스
목걸이

necklace necklace necklace

need
[ni:d] 니-드
필요하다

need need need need

neighbor

[néibər] 네이버

이웃

neighbor neighbor neighbor

never

[névər] 네버

결코 ~않다

never never never never

noise

[nɔiz] 노이즈

소리, 소음

noise noise noise noise

not

[nát] 낱

않다, 아니다

not not not not not

nothing

[nʌ́θiŋ] 너씽

아무것도 ~아니다

nothing nothing nothing

off
[ɔ:f] 오-프
~에서 떨어져

off   off   off   off   off

officer
[ɔ́:fisər] 오피서
장교, 공무원

officer   officer   officer   officer

often
[ɔ́:ftn] 오픈
종종, 자주

often   often   often   often

or
[ɔ:r] 오-
또는, 혹은

or   or   or   or   or   or

other
[ʌðər] 어더
다른, 타인

other   other   other   other

pain
[pein] 페인
통증

pain　pain　pain　pain

pair
[pɛər] 페어
한 쌍, 한 벌

pair　pair　pair　pair

past
[pæst] 패스트
지나간

past　past　past　past

pay
[pei] 페이
지불하다

pay　pay　pay　pay

pepper
[pépər] 페퍼
후추

pepper　pepper　pepper

pilot
[páilət] 파일럳

조종사, 파일럿

pilot   pilot   pilot   pilot

pleasant
[pléznt] 플레즌트

즐거운

pleasant   pleasant   pleasant

please
[pli:z] 플리-즈

기쁘게 하다

please   please   please

polite
[pəláit] 펄라이트

예의 바른

polite   polite   polite

poor
[puər] 푸어

가난한

poor   poor   poor   poor

practice
[prǽktis] 프랙티스

연습, 연습하다

practice　　practice　　practice

president
[prézidənt] 프레지던트

대통령

president　president　president

promise
[prámis] 프라미스

약속하다

promise　　promise　　promise

question
[kwéstʃən] 퀘스천

질문

question　　question　　question

quick
[kwik] 퀵

빠른

quick　quick　quick　quick

quiet
[kwáiət] 콰이엍

조용한

quiet quiet quiet quiet

raise
[reiz] 레이즈

올리다, 기르다

raise raise raise raise

receive
[risíːv] 리시-브

받다

receive receive receive

rectangle
[réktæŋgl] 렉탱글

직사각형

rectangle rectangle rectangle

relax
[rilǽks] 릴랙스

긴장을 풀다

relax relax relax relax

6학년 · Day 19

remember
[rimémbər] 리멤버
기억하다

remember remember remember

repeat
[ripíːt] 리피—트
반복하다

repeat repeat repeat repeat

reply
[riplái] 리플라이
대답하다

reply reply reply reply

report
[ripɔ́ːrt] 리포—트
보고, 보고서

report report report report

ride
[raid] 라이드
타다

ride ride ride ride ride

round
[raund] 라운드
둥근

round   round   round   round

rule
[ru:l] 루-ㄹ
규칙

rule   rule   rule   rule

same
[seim] 세임
같은

same   same   same   same

sandwich
[sǽnwitʃ] 샌위치
샌드위치

sandwich   sandwich   sandwich

scissors
[sízərz] 시저즈
가위

scissors   scissors   scissors   scissors

search

[səːrtʃ] 써-취

찾다

search   search   search   search

season

[síːzn] 씨-즌

계절

season   season   season   season

secret

[síːkrit] 씨-크릿

비밀

secret   secret   secret   secret

shade

[ʃeid] 쉐이드

그늘

shade   shade   shade   shade

shadow

[ʃǽdou] 쉐도우

그림자

shadow   shadow   shadow

shake
[ʃeik] 쉐이크
흔들다

shake shake shake shake

shape
[ʃeip] 쉐이프
모양, 형태

shape shape shape shape

shoulder
[ʃóuldər] 쇼울더
어깨

shoulder shoulder shoulder

shout
[ʃaut] 샤우트
외치다

shout shout shout shout

shower
[ʃáuər] 샤워
샤워, 소나기

shower shower shower

side
[said] 사이드

옆, 측면

side　side　side　side

smoke
[smouk] 스모욱

연기, 흡연

smoke　smoke　smoke　smoke

so
[sou] 소우

그래서

so　so　so　so　so　so

something
[sʌ́mθiŋ] 썸씽

어떤 것, 무엇

something　something

sometimes
[sʌ́mtàimz] 썸타임즈

가끔

sometimes　sometimes

soon
[suːn] 쑨-
곧

soon   soon   soon   soon

special
[spéʃəl] 스페셜
특별한

special   special   special   special

spell
[spel] 스펠
철자를 쓰다

spell   spell   spell   spell

spend
[spend] 스펜드
지출하다, 쓰다

spend   spend   spend   spend

spider
[spáidər] 스파이더
거미

spider   spider   spider   spider

square
[skwɛər] 스퀘어

정사각형

square square square

stick
[stik] 스틱

막대기

stick stick stick stick

stomach
[stʌ́mək] 스터먹

위, 배

stomach stomach stomach

stomachache
[stʌ́məkèik] 스터먹에익

복통, 배앓이

stomachache stomachache

storm
[stɔːrm] 스토-ㅁ

폭풍우

storm storm storm storm

straight
[streit] 스트레이트

똑바로, 곧장

straight   straight   straight

surprise
[sərpráiz] 서프라이즈

놀라다

surprise   surprise   surprise

surprising
[sərpráiziŋ] 서프라이징

놀라운

surprising   surprising   surprising

table tennis
[téibl tènis] 테이블 테니스

탁구

table tennis   table tennis

than
[ðǽn] 댄

~보다

than   than   than   than

theater

[θíːətər] 씨어터

극장

theater theater theater

then

[ðen] 덴

그때

then then then then

these

[ðiːz] 디ㅡ즈

이것들

these these these these

they

[ðei] 데이

그들

they they they they

thin

[θin] 씬

얇은, 마른

thin thin thin thin

thirsty
[θə́ːrsti] 써-스티
목마른

thirsty thirsty thirsty thirsty

those
[ðouz] 도우즈
저것들

those those those those

throw
[θrou] 쓰로우
던지다

throw throw throw throw

tooth
[tuːθ] 투-쓰
치아

tooth tooth tooth tooth

toothache
[túːθèik] 투-쓰에익
치통

toothache toothache

triangle

[tráiæŋgl] 트라이앵글

삼각형

triangle   triangle   triangle

trip

[trip] 트립

여행

trip   trip   trip   trip

trouble

[trʌ́bl] 트러블

문제

trouble   trouble   trouble

true

[truː] 트루-

사실인, 맞는

true   true   true   true

turkey

[tə́ːrki] 터-키

칠면조

turkey   turkey   turkey

ugly
[ʌ́gli] 어글리
못생긴

ugly　　ugly　　ugly　　ugly

umbrella
[ʌmbrélə] 엄브렐러
우산

umbrella　umbrella　umbrella

understand
[ʌ́ndərstǽnd] 언더스탠드
이해하다

understand　understand

until
[əntíl] 언틸
~까지

until　　until　　until　　until

usually
[júːʒuəli] 유-주얼리
보통, 대개

usually　usually　usually

wallet
[wάlit] 왈릿
지갑

wallet wallet wallet wallet

war
[wɔːr] 워-
전쟁

war war war war

warm
[wɔːrm] 워-엄
따뜻한

warm warm warm warm

weak
[wiːk] 위-크
약한

weak weak weak weak

weight
[weit] 웨이트
무게

weight weight weight weight

will

[wíl] 윌

~일 것이다

will   will   will   will

wise

[waiz] 와이즈

현명한

wise   wise   wise   wise

worry

[wə́:ri] 워-리

걱정하다

worry   worry   worry   worry

worse

[wə:rs] 워-스

더 나쁜

worse   worse   worse   worse

yet

[jet] 옡

아직

yet yet yet yet yet yet

재미있는 **영단어 퀴즈**

1 아래 그림을 보고 빈칸을 채워 영단어를 완성하세요.

1) _ _ lon

2) buc _ _ _ _

3) f _ _ tory

4) _ _ brella

5) isla _ _

6) b _ _ ch

2 아래 보기에서 알맞은 우리말을 찾아 쓰세요.

> **보기**
>
> 남편 폭풍우 충고 대통령 움직이다 대답하다

1) storm _____

4) advice _____

2) reply _____

5) husband _____

3) president _____

6) move _____

3 우리말에 맞게 영단어를 바르게 써 보세요.

보기

d n g r a e ➡ 위험 _danger_

1) a r w

전쟁 _____

4) o f g

안개 _____

2) s m e a

같은 _____

5) h r d a

딱딱한 _____

3) l u a g h

웃다 _____

6) s k m e o

연기 _____

4 영단어에 알맞은 우리말을 줄로 연결하세요.

1) season ·   · 국가

2) matter ·   · 계절

3) history ·   · 문제

4) nation ·   · 역사

5 우리말에 알맞은 영단어를 쓰고 퍼즐을 완성하세요.

힌트

meal　baseball　pilot
secret　trip　quiet

비밀

야구　e

조용한　e

조종사

식사　l

여행　t

222

부록

- 반대말
- 날짜와 시간, 숫자
- 초등 필수 영단어 사전

반대말

arrive	도착하다	departure	출발하다
ask	묻다	answer	답하다
asleep	잠든	awake	깨어 있는
attack	공격	defence	방어
beautiful	아름다운	ugly	미운
best	가장 좋은	worst	가장 나쁜
big	큰	small	작은
bright	밝은	dark	어두운
buy	사다	sell	팔다
clean	깨끗한	dirty	더러운
day	낮	night	밤
deep	깊은	low	얕은
dry	마른	wet	젖은
early	이른	late	늦은
easy	쉬운	difficult	어려운
fast	빠른	slow	느린
fat	뚱뚱한	thin	마른
find	찾다	lose	잃다
first	처음	last	마지막
front	앞	back	뒤
full	가득 찬	empty	텅 빈
good	좋은	bad	나쁜
happy	행복한	sad	슬픈
heavy	무거운	light	가벼운
high	높은	low	낮은
hot	더운	cold	추운

in	안	out	밖
joy	기쁨	sorrow	슬픔
live	살다	die	죽다
long	긴	short	짧은
more	더	less	덜
near	가까운	far	먼
old	낡은	new	새로운
open	열다	close	닫다
push	밀다	pull	당기다
quick	빠른	slow	느린
quiet	조용한	noisy	시끄러운
rich	부유한	poor	가난한
right	오른쪽	left	왼쪽
simple	단순한	complex	복잡한
smart	똑똑한	foolish	어리석은
soft	부드러운	hard	딱딱한
special	특별한	general	일반적인
strong	강한	weak	약한
sweet	달콤한	bitter	쓴
tall	키가 큰	short	키가 작은
thin	얇은	thick	두꺼운
true	진실의	false	거짓의
up	위	down	아래
victory	승리	defeat	패배
white	흰	black	검은
wide	넓은	narrow	좁은
win	이기다	lose	지다
yes	네	no	아니요
young	젊은	old	늙은

날짜와 시간, 숫자

날짜와 시간

[월]

January	1월
February	2월
March	3월
April	4월
May	5월
June	6월
July	7월
August	8월
September	9월
October	10월
November	11월
December	12월

[요일]

Monday	월요일
Tuesday	화요일
Wednesday	수요일
Thursday	목요일
Friday	금요일
Saturday	토요일
Sunday	일요일

[시간]

year	년, 해
month	달, 월
week	주, 일주일
weekday	평일
weekend	주말
day	하루
hour	1시간
minute	분
second	초
o' clock	o' clock (정각) ~시
morning	아침, 오전
noon	정오, 낮 12시
evening	저녁
night	밤, 야간

기수 기본이 되는 수		**서수** 순서를 나타내는 수		

기수		서수	
one	1	first	1번째
two	2	second	2번째
three	3	third	3번째
four	4	fourth	4번째
five	5	fifth	5번째
six	6	sixth	6번째
seven	7	seventh	7번째
eight	8	eighth	8번째
nine	9	ninth	9번째
ten	10	tenth	10번째
eleven	11	eleventh	11번째
twelve	12	twelfth	12번째
thirteen	13	thirteenth	13번째
fourteen	14	fourteenth	14번째
fifteen	15	fifteenth	15번째
sixteen	16	sixteenth	16번째
seventeen	17	seventeenth	17번째
eighteen	18	eighteenth	18번째
nineteen	19	nineteenth	19번째
twenty	20	twentieth	20번째
thirty	30	thirtieth	30번째
forty	40	fortieth	40번째
fitty	50	fiftieth	50번째
sixty	60	sixtieth	60번째
seventy	70	seventieth	70번째
eighty	80	eightieth	80번째
ninety	90	ninetieth	90번째
hundred	100	hundredth	100번째
thousand	1000	thousandth	1000번째

초등 필수 영단어 사전

* 암기한 단어에 V표시 하면서 초등 필수 영단어를 복습하세요!

A

□ able	~할 수 있는
□ about	~에 대한
□ absent	결석한
□ accident	사고
□ act	행동하다
□ action	행동
□ actor	배우
□ actress	여배우
□ address	주소
□ advice	충고, 조언
□ after	~ 뒤에, ~ 후에
□ afternoon	오후
□ again	다시
□ age	나이
□ ago	~ 전에
□ agree	동의하다
□ ahead	앞에, 앞으로
□ air	공기
□ airplane	비행기
□ airport	공항
□ album	앨범
□ all	모든
□ allow	허락하다
□ almost	거의
□ alone	혼자
□ alphabet	알파벳
□ already	이미
□ also	또한, 역시
□ always	항상
□ and	그리고, ~와
□ angry	화난
□ animal	동물
□ another	또 하나의
□ answer	대답, 답하다
□ ant	개미
□ any	어떤, 어느
□ anything	무엇이든, 아무것도
□ anyway	어쨌든
□ apple	사과
□ April	4월

□ arm	팔
□ army	군대
□ around	주위에
□ arrive	도착하다
□ art	예술, 미술
□ artist	예술가
□ ask	묻다
□ at	~에
□ attend	출석하다
□ August	8월
□ aunt	이모, 고모
□ autumn	가을
□ away	떨어져

B

□ baby	아기
□ back	뒤, 등
□ backyard	뒤뜰
□ bad	나쁜
□ badminton	배드민턴
□ bag	가방
□ ball	공
□ balloon	풍선
□ banana	바나나
□ bank	은행
□ base	기초, 토대
□ baseball	야구
□ basket	바구니
□ basketball	농구
□ bat	박쥐, 방망이
□ bath	목욕
□ bathroom	욕실
□ beach	해변
□ bear	곰
□ beautiful	아름다운
□ because	~ 때문에, 왜냐하면
□ become	~이 되다
□ bed	침대
□ bedroom	침실
□ bee	벌

□ beef	소고기	□ building	건물
□ before	~ 전에	□ bus	버스
□ begin	시작하다	□ busy	바쁜
□ behind	~ 뒤에	□ but	그러나
□ believe	믿다	□ butter	버터
□ bell	벨, 종	□ button	단추
□ belt	허리띠	□ buy	사다
□ bench	벤치, 긴 의자	□ by	~ 옆에
□ best	최고의	□ bye	잘 가, 안녕
□ better	더 좋은		
□ between	~ 사이에	**C**	
□ bicycle	자전거		
□ big	큰	□ cake	케이크
□ bike	자전거	□ calendar	달력
□ bird	새	□ call	전화하다
□ birthday	생일	□ camera	카메라
□ black	검은색	□ camping	캠핑, 야영
□ blackboard	칠판	□ can	할 수 있다
□ blanket	이불	□ candle	양초
□ block	블록	□ candy	사탕
□ blood	피, 혈액	□ cap	모자
□ blossom	꽃, 꽃피다	□ captain	선장, 장
□ blouse	블라우스	□ car	자동차
□ blue	파란색	□ card	카드
□ boat	배, 보트	□ careful	조심스러운, 주의 깊은
□ body	몸	□ carrot	당근
□ book	책	□ carry	나르다
□ bookcase	책장	□ case	상자, 통
□ bookstore	서점	□ cat	고양이
□ boots	부츠, 장화	□ catch	잡다
□ both	둘 다	□ cave	동굴
□ bottle	병	□ ceiling	천장
□ bottom	밑, 밑바닥	□ center	중심, 중앙
□ bowl	그릇	□ chair	의자
□ box	상자	□ chalk	분필
□ boy	남자 아이, 소년	□ chance	기회, 가능성
□ bread	빵	□ change	변하다, 바꾸다
□ break	깨다, 부수다	□ cheap	(값이) 싼
□ breakfast	아침 식사	□ check	확인하다
□ bridge	다리	□ cheek	볼, 뺨
□ bright	밝은	□ cheese	치즈
□ bring	가져오다, 데려오다	□ chicken	닭
□ broad	넓은	□ child	아이, 어린이
□ brother	형, 오빠, 남동생	□ chocolate	초콜릿
□ brown	갈색	□ choose	선택하다
□ brush	빗, 솔, 빗질하다	□ chopstick	젓가락
□ bucket	양동이	□ Christmas	크리스마스
□ build	짓다, 세우다	□ church	교회

□ circle	원, 동그라미		□ dad	아빠
□ city	도시		□ dance	춤추다
□ class	학급, 수업		□ danger	위험
□ classmate	동급생, 반 친구		□ dark	어두운
□ classroom	교실		□ date	날짜

□ circle	원, 동그라미
□ city	도시
□ class	학급, 수업
□ classmate	동급생, 반 친구
□ classroom	교실
□ clean	청소하다, 깨끗한
□ clear	맑은
□ clever	영리한
□ clock	시계
□ close	닫다
□ cloth	천
□ clothes	옷, 의상
□ cloud	구름
□ cloudy	구름 낀
□ coat	외투
□ coin	동전
□ cold	차가운, 추운
□ collect	모으다
□ color	색깔
□ come	오다
□ company	회사
□ computer	컴퓨터
□ concert	공연
□ condition	상태, 조건
□ cone	원뿔
□ congratulate	축하하다
□ continue	계속하다
□ cook	요리하다
□ cookie	쿠키
□ cool	시원한
□ copy	복사, 모방
□ corn	옥수수
□ corner	구석, 모퉁이
□ correct	정확한
□ cost	비용, 대가
□ count	세다, 계산하다
□ country	나라, 국가
□ course	코스, 과정
□ cousin	사촌
□ cover	덮다, 씌우다
□ cow	소
□ crayon	크레용
□ cross	건너다, 가로지르다
□ cry	울다
□ cup	컵
□ curtain	커튼
□ cut	자르다
□ cute	귀여운

D

□ dad	아빠
□ dance	춤추다
□ danger	위험
□ dark	어두운
□ date	날짜
□ daughter	딸
□ dear	사랑하는, 소중한
□ December	12월
□ deep	깊은, 짙은
□ deer	사슴
□ delicious	맛있는
□ dentist	치과 의사
□ desk	책상
□ diary	일기
□ dictionary	사전
□ die	죽다
□ different	다른
□ difficult	어려운
□ dinner	저녁 식사
□ dirty	더러운
□ dish	접시
□ do	～하다
□ doctor	의사
□ dog	개
□ doll	인형
□ dollar	달러
□ dolphin	돌고래
□ door	문
□ double	두 배의
□ down	아래로
□ draw	그리다
□ dream	꿈, 희망
□ dress	드레스, 옷
□ drink	마시다
□ drive	운전하다
□ driver	운전사
□ drop	떨어지다
□ dry	마른, 말리다
□ duck	오리

E

□ ear	귀
□ earache	귀앓이
□ early	일찍, 이른
□ earth	지구, 땅, 흙

□ east	동쪽	□ field	들판, 밭
□ easy	쉬운	□ fifth	5번째
□ eat	먹다	□ fight	싸우다
□ egg	달걀	□ fill	채우다
□ eight	8, 여덟	□ film	필름, 영화
□ eighth	8번째	□ find	찾다
□ elementary	기초의, 초등의	□ fine	좋은
□ elephant	코끼리	□ finger	손가락
□ elevator	엘리베이터	□ finish	끝내다, 마치다
□ empty	비어 있는	□ fire	불
□ end	끝, 끝내다	□ first	1번째
□ English	영어	□ fish	물고기
□ enjoy	즐기다	□ five	5, 다섯
□ enough	충분한	□ fix	고치다, 고정하다
□ enter	~에 들어가다	□ flag	깃발, 기
□ eraser	지우개	□ floor	바닥, 층
□ evening	저녁	□ flower	꽃
□ event	행사, 이벤트	□ fly	날다
□ every	모든	□ fog	안개
□ everyone	모든 사람	□ foggy	안개가 낀
□ everywhere	어디나, 모든 곳	□ follow	따르다, 뒤를 잇다
□ example	예	□ food	음식
□ excellent	훌륭한	□ fool	바보
□ excite	흥분시키다	□ foolish	바보 같은
□ exciting	신나는, 흥미진진한	□ foot	발
□ excuse	용서하다	□ football	축구
□ expensive	비싼	□ for	~을 위해
□ eye	눈	□ forest	숲
		□ forget	잊다
		□ fork	포크
F		□ four	4, 넷
		□ fourth	4번째
□ face	얼굴	□ fox	여우
□ fact	사실	□ free	자유로운
□ factory	공장	□ fresh	신선한
□ fall	떨어지다	□ Friday	금요일
□ family	가족	□ friend	친구
□ fan	선풍기	□ frog	개구리
□ far	멀리	□ from	~부터
□ farm	농장	□ front	앞, 정면
□ farmer	농부	□ fruit	과일
□ fast	빠른	□ full	가득 찬
□ fat	살찐, 뚱뚱한	□ fun	재미, 재미있는
□ father	아버지	□ funny	우스운, 웃기는
□ favorite	매우 좋아하는	□ future	미래
□ February	2월		
□ feed	먹이, 먹이를 주다		
□ feel	느끼다		
□ few	(수가) 적은		

G

□ game	게임, 경기
□ garden	정원
□ gas	가스, 기체
□ gate	문, 대문
□ gather	모이다
□ gentle	순한, 온화한
□ gentleman	신사
□ get	얻다
□ gift	선물
□ giraffe	기린
□ girl	소녀
□ give	주다
□ glad	기쁜
□ glass	유리, 유리컵
□ glove	장갑
□ glue	풀
□ go	가다
□ goat	염소
□ gold	금색
□ goldfish	금붕어
□ good	좋은
□ granddaughter	손녀
□ grandfather	할아버지
□ grandmother	할머니
□ grandson	손자
□ grape	포도
□ grass	잔디, 풀
□ gray	회색
□ great	위대한, 큰
□ green	초록색
□ ground	지면, 땅
□ group	그룹, 단체
□ grow	자라다
□ guess	추측하다
□ guide	길잡이, 안내자
□ guitar	기타

H

□ habit	버릇, 습관
□ hair	머리카락
□ half	반, 절반
□ hall	홀, 집회장
□ hamburger	햄버거
□ hand	손
□ handsome	멋진, 잘생긴

□ hang	걸다, 매달리다
□ happy	행복한
□ hard	딱딱한, 어려운
□ harvest	추수하다
□ hat	모자
□ hate	미워하다
□ have	가지다, 먹다
□ he	그
□ head	머리
□ headache	두통
□ health	건강
□ hear	듣다
□ heart	심장, 가슴
□ heat	열, 더위
□ heavy	무거운
□ helicopter	헬리콥터
□ hello	안녕하세요
□ help	돕다
□ hen	암탉
□ here	여기
□ hi	안녕
□ hide	숨기다, 감추다
□ high	높은
□ hiking	하이킹, 보도 여행
□ hill	언덕
□ history	역사
□ hit	치다, 때리다
□ hobby	취미
□ hold	잡다, 쥐다
□ hole	구멍
□ holiday	휴일, 휴가
□ home	집
□ homework	숙제
□ honest	정직한
□ honey	꿀, 여보
□ hope	바라다
□ horse	말
□ hospital	병원
□ hot	뜨거운, 더운
□ hotel	호텔
□ hour	1시간, 시간
□ house	집
□ how	어떻게
□ hungry	배고픈
□ hurry	서두르다
□ hurt	다친, 아프다
□ husband	남편

I

□ I	나
□ ice	얼음
□ ice cream	아이스크림
□ idea	생각, 아이디어
□ if	만약 ~라면
□ ill	아픈
□ important	중요한
□ in	~ 안에
□ insect	곤충
□ inside	안쪽, 내부
□ interesting	재미있는, 흥미로운
□ into	~ 안으로
□ introduce	소개하다
□ invite	초대하다
□ island	섬
□ it	그것

J

□ January	1월
□ jeans	청바지
□ job	직업
□ join	참여하다, 가입하다
□ joy	기쁨, 즐거움
□ juice	주스
□ July	7월
□ jump	뛰다, 점프하다
□ June	6월
□ jungle	정글, 밀림
□ just	막

K

□ kangaroo	캥거루
□ keep	계속하다
□ key	열쇠
□ kick	차다, 킥
□ kid	아이
□ kill	죽이다
□ kind	친절한
□ king	왕
□ kitchen	주방
□ kitty	새끼 고양이
□ knee	무릎
□ knife	칼
□ knock	두드리다

□ know	알다
□ Korea	한국, 대한민국

L

□ lady	여성, 숙녀
□ lake	호수
□ lamb	어린 양
□ lamp	램프, 전등
□ land	땅, 육지
□ language	언어
□ large	넓은
□ last	지난
□ late	늦은
□ laugh	웃다
□ laundry	세탁물, 세탁
□ law	법
□ lazy	게으른
□ lead	이끌다
□ leader	지도자
□ leaf	나뭇잎
□ learn	배우다
□ leave	떠나다
□ left	왼쪽
□ leg	다리
□ lend	빌려주다
□ lesson	수업, 연습
□ let's	~하자
□ letter	편지
□ level	레벨, 수준
□ library	도서관
□ lie	거짓말, 눕다
□ life	인생, 삶
□ lift	올리다, 승강기
□ light	빛, 가벼운
□ like	좋아하다
□ line	줄
□ lion	사자
□ lip	입술
□ list	목록
□ listen	듣다
□ little	작은
□ live	살다
□ living room	거실
□ lock	잠그다
□ lonely	외로운
□ long	긴
□ look	보다

□ lose	잃다, 지다		□ morning	아침
□ loss	잃음, 손해		□ most	대부분
□ loud	시끄러운		□ mother	어머니
□ love	사랑, 사랑하다		□ mountain	산
□ low	낮은		□ mouse	쥐
□ lucky	운이 좋은		□ mouth	입
□ lunch	점심 식사		□ move	움직이다
			□ movie	영화
M			□ much	(양이) 많은
			□ museum	박물관
□ machine	기계		□ music	음악
□ magazine	잡지		□ musical	뮤지컬
□ mail	우편		□ musician	음악가
□ make	만들다		□ must	~해야 한다
□ man	(성인) 남자			
□ many	(수가) 많은		**N**	
□ map	지도			
□ March	3월		□ name	이름
□ market	시장		□ narrow	좁은
□ marry	결혼하다		□ nation	국가, 국민
□ match	경기, 시합		□ nature	자연
□ math	수학		□ near	근처, 가까운
□ matter	문제, 일		□ neck	목
□ may	~일지도 모른다		□ necklace	목걸이
□ May	5월		□ need	필요하다
□ meal	식사		□ neighbor	이웃
□ mean	의미하다		□ nest	둥지
□ meat	고기		□ never	결코 ~ 않다
□ meet	만나다		□ new	새로운
□ meeting	만남, 회의		□ news	뉴스, 보도
□ melon	멜론		□ newspaper	신문
□ middle	중앙, 가운데		□ next	다음의, 옆의
□ milk	우유		□ nice	좋은
□ mind	마음		□ night	밤
□ minus	빼기, 빼다		□ nine	9, 아홉
□ minute	분		□ ninth	9번째
□ mirror	거울		□ no	없다, 아니다
□ miss	놓치다		□ noise	소리, 소음
□ mistake	실수		□ north	북쪽
□ mix	섞다		□ nose	코
□ model	모델, 모형		□ not	않다, 아니다
□ mom	엄마		□ note	메모
□ Monday	월요일		□ notebook	노트, 공책
□ money	돈		□ nothing	아무것도 ~ 아니다
□ monkey	원숭이		□ November	11월
□ month	달, 월		□ now	지금, 현재
□ moon	달		□ number	숫자
□ more	좀 더		□ nurse	간호사

O

□ o'clock	(정각) ~시
□ ocean	바다, 대양
□ October	10월
□ of	~의
□ off	~에서 떨어져
□ office	사무실
□ officer	장교, 공무원
□ often	종종, 자주
□ oil	기름
□ OK	좋아
□ old	늙은, 오래된
□ on	~ 위에
□ once	한 번
□ one	1, 하나
□ onion	양파
□ only	유일한, 단 하나의
□ oops	이크, 이런
□ open	열다
□ or	또는, 혹은
□ orange	오렌지
□ other	다른, 타인
□ out	~ 밖에
□ outside	밖
□ over	~ 위에

P

□ page	페이지, 쪽
□ pain	통증
□ paint	그리다, 페인트
□ pair	한 쌍, 한 벌
□ pants	바지
□ paper	종이
□ parent	부모
□ park	공원
□ part	부분, 일부
□ party	파티
□ pass	통과하다
□ past	지나간
□ pay	지불하다
□ peach	복숭아
□ pear	배
□ pen	펜
□ pencil	연필
□ pencil case	필통
□ people	사람들

□ pepper	후추
□ perfect	완벽한
□ person	사람
□ pet	애완동물
□ photo	사진
□ piano	피아노
□ pick	고르다
□ picnic	소풍
□ picture	그림, 사진
□ pie	파이
□ piece	조각
□ pig	돼지
□ pilot	조종사, 파일럿
□ pineapple	파인애플
□ pink	분홍색
□ place	장소
□ plan	계획, 계획하다
□ plane	비행기
□ plant	식물
□ play	놀다
□ pleasant	즐거운
□ please	기쁘게 하다
□ plus	더하기, 더하다
□ pocket	주머니
□ point	요점, 가리키다
□ police	경찰
□ polite	예의 바른
□ pool	수영장, 풀
□ poor	가난한
□ post	우편
□ post office	우체국
□ poster	포스터
□ pot	냄비
□ potato	감자
□ power	권력, 힘
□ practice	연습, 연습하다
□ present	선물
□ president	대통령
□ press	누르다
□ pretty	예쁜, 귀여운
□ price	값, 가격
□ prince	왕자
□ princess	공주
□ print	인쇄하다
□ problem	문제
□ promise	약속하다
□ pull	끌다, 당기다
□ puppy	강아지

□ pure	순수한	□ room	방
□ purple	보라색	□ round	둥근
□ push	밀다	□ rule	규칙
□ put	두다, 놓다	□ ruler	자
		□ run	달리다

Q

□ queen	여왕		
□ question	질문		
□ quick	빠른		
□ quiet	조용한		

S

□ sad	슬픈
□ safe	안전한
□ salad	샐러드
□ salt	소금
□ same	같은
□ sand	모래
□ sandwich	샌드위치
□ Saturday	토요일
□ save	저축하다, 절약하다
□ say	말하다
□ school	학교
□ science	과학
□ scientist	과학자
□ scissors	가위
□ score	점수
□ sea	바다
□ search	찾다
□ season	계절
□ seat	자리, 좌석
□ second	2번째, 초
□ secret	비밀
□ see	보다
□ sell	팔다
□ send	보내다
□ September	9월
□ service	서비스, 봉사
□ set	놓다, 두다
□ seven	7, 일곱
□ seventh	7번째
□ shade	그늘
□ shadow	그림자
□ shake	흔들다
□ shape	모양, 형태
□ she	그녀
□ sheep	양
□ ship	배
□ shirt	셔츠
□ shoes	신발
□ shop	상점, 가게
□ shopping	쇼핑

R

□ rabbit	토끼
□ race	경주, 경기
□ radio	라디오
□ rain	비
□ rainbow	무지개
□ rainy	비가 오는
□ raise	올리다, 기르다
□ read	읽다
□ ready	준비된
□ real	진짜의, 진실의
□ really	정말로
□ receive	받다
□ rectangle	직사각형
□ red	빨간색
□ relax	긴장을 풀다
□ remember	기억하다
□ repeat	반복하다
□ reply	대답하다
□ report	보고, 보고서
□ rest	휴식
□ restaurant	식당
□ restroom	화장실
□ review	복습하다
□ ribbon	리본
□ rice	쌀, 밥
□ rich	부유한
□ ride	타다
□ right	옳은
□ ring	반지
□ river	강
□ road	도로, 길
□ robot	로봇
□ rock	바위
□ roof	지붕

☐ short	짧은		☐ speak	말하다
☐ shoulder	어깨		☐ special	특별한
☐ shout	외치다		☐ speech	연설
☐ show	보여주다		☐ speed	속도
☐ shower	샤워, 소나기		☐ spell	철자를 쓰다
☐ sick	아픈		☐ spend	지출하다, 쓰다
☐ side	옆, 측면		☐ spider	거미
☐ sign	간판, 서명하다		☐ spoon	숟가락
☐ silver	은, 은색의		☐ sport	스포츠
☐ simple	간단한		☐ spring	봄
☐ sing	노래하다		☐ square	정사각형
☐ singer	가수		☐ stair	계단
☐ sir	~씨, ~님		☐ stamp	도장
☐ sister	언니, 누나, 여동생		☐ stand	서다
☐ sit	앉다		☐ star	별
☐ six	6, 여섯		☐ start	시작하다
☐ sixth	6번째		☐ station	역
☐ size	크기, 치수		☐ stay	머물다
☐ skate	스케이트		☐ step	걸음, 단계
☐ ski	스키		☐ stick	막대기
☐ skirt	치마		☐ stomach	위, 배
☐ sky	하늘		☐ stomachache	복통, 배앓이
☐ sleep	자다		☐ stone	돌
☐ slow	느린		☐ stop	멈추다
☐ small	작은		☐ store	가게, 상점
☐ smell	냄새가 나다		☐ storm	폭풍우
☐ smile	미소		☐ story	이야기
☐ smoke	연기, 흡연		☐ straight	똑바로, 곧장
☐ snake	뱀		☐ strawberry	딸기
☐ snow	눈		☐ street	거리, 도로
☐ snowman	눈사람		☐ strong	강한, 힘센
☐ so	그래서		☐ student	학생
☐ soap	비누		☐ study	공부하다
☐ soccer	축구		☐ style	스타일, 방식
☐ sock	양말		☐ subway	지하철
☐ sofa	소파		☐ sugar	설탕
☐ soft	부드러운		☐ summer	여름
☐ some	일부, 약간의		☐ sun	해, 태양
☐ something	어떤 것, 무엇		☐ Sunday	일요일
☐ sometimes	가끔		☐ sunny	맑은, 화창한
☐ son	아들		☐ sure	물론
☐ song	노래		☐ surprise	놀라다
☐ soon	곧		☐ surprising	놀라운
☐ sorry	미안한		☐ sweater	스웨터
☐ sound	소리		☐ sweet	달콤한
☐ soup	수프		☐ swim	수영하다
☐ south	남쪽			
☐ space	공간, 우주			

T

□ table	탁자
□ table tennis	탁구
□ tail	꼬리
□ take	잡다
□ talk	말하다
□ tall	키가 큰
□ tape	테이프
□ taxi	택시
□ tea	차
□ teach	가르치다
□ teacher	선생님
□ team	팀, 단체
□ telephone	전화
□ tell	말하다
□ ten	10, 열
□ tennis	테니스
□ tent	텐트
□ tenth	10번째
□ test	시험
□ textbook	교과서
□ than	~보다
□ thank	감사하다
□ that	저것
□ theater	극장
□ then	그때
□ there	거기에
□ these	이것들
□ they	그들
□ thin	얇은, 마른
□ think	생각하다
□ third	3번째
□ thirsty	목마른
□ this	이것
□ those	저것들
□ three	3, 셋
□ throw	던지다
□ Thursday	목요일
□ ticket	표, 티켓
□ tie	넥타이, 묶다
□ tiger	호랑이
□ time	시간
□ tired	피곤한
□ to	~로, ~쪽으로
□ today	오늘
□ toe	발가락
□ together	함께

□ toilet	화장실, 변기
□ tomato	토마토
□ tomorrow	내일
□ tonight	오늘밤
□ too	또한, 너무
□ tooth	치아
□ toothache	치통
□ top	꼭대기, 정상
□ touch	만지다
□ towel	수건
□ tower	탑
□ town	마을, 동네
□ toy	장난감
□ traffic	교통
□ train	기차
□ travel	여행하다, 여행
□ tree	나무
□ triangle	삼각형
□ trip	여행
□ trouble	문제
□ true	사실인, 맞는
□ try	노력하다
□ Tuesday	화요일
□ turkey	칠면조
□ turn	돌다
□ two	2, 둘

U

□ ugly	못생긴
□ umbrella	우산
□ uncle	삼촌
□ under	~ 아래에
□ understand	이해하다
□ uniform	제복, 유니폼
□ until	~까지
□ up	위로
□ use	사용하다
□ usually	보통, 대개

V

□ vacation	방학, 휴가
□ vegetable	채소
□ very	매우, 대단히
□ view	경치, 전망
□ village	마을
□ violin	바이올린

□ visit   방문하다
□ voice   목소리

W

□ wait   기다리다
□ wake   (잠에서) 깨다
□ walk   걷다
□ wall   벽
□ wallet   지갑
□ want   원하다
□ war   전쟁
□ warm   따뜻한
□ wash   씻다
□ watch   손목시계, 보다
□ water   물
□ watermelon   수박
□ wave   파도
□ way   길, 방법
□ we   우리
□ weak   약한
□ wear   입다
□ weather   날씨
□ Wednesday   수요일
□ week   주, 일주일
□ weekday   평일
□ weekend   주말
□ weight   무게
□ welcome   환영하다
□ well   잘, 좋게
□ west   서쪽
□ wet   젖은, 축축한
□ what   무엇
□ when   언제
□ where   어디
□ white   흰색
□ who   누구
□ why   왜
□ wide   넓은
□ wife   아내, 부인
□ will   ~일 것이다
□ win   이기다
□ wind   바람
□ window   창문
□ windy   바람 부는
□ wing   날개
□ winter   겨울
□ wise   현명한

□ wish   원하다
□ with   ~와 함께
□ wolf   늑대
□ woman   (성인) 여자
□ wonderful   훌륭한
□ wood   나무, 목재
□ word   단어, 낱말
□ work   일하다
□ world   세계, 세상
□ worry   걱정하다
□ worse   더 나쁜
□ wow   야, 와
□ write   쓰다
□ wrong   틀린, 잘못된

X

□ x-ray   엑스레이

Y

□ yard   마당, 뜰
□ year   년, 해
□ yellow   노란색
□ yes   네, 그래
□ yesterday   어제
□ yet   아직
□ you   너
□ young   어린, 젊은

Z

□ zebra   얼룩말
□ zoo   동물원

지은이 키즈키즈 교육연구소

기획과 편집, 창작 활동을 전문으로 하는 유아동 교육연구소입니다.
어린이들이 건강한 생각을 키우고 올곧은 인성을 세우는 데 도움이 되는
교육 콘텐츠를 개발하고 있습니다. 즐기면서 배울 수 있는 프로그램 개발에도
힘쓰고 있으며, 단행본과 학습지 등 다양한 분야에서 활동하고 있습니다.

하루10분
초등영단어
따라쓰기

3~6학년 영단어 한 권으로 끝내기

중쇄 인쇄 | 2024년 12월 24일
중쇄 발행 | 2024년 12월 30일

지은이 | 키즈키즈 교육연구소
펴낸이 | 박수길
펴낸곳 | (주)도서출판 미래지식
기획 편집 | 이솔
디자인 | design Ko

주소 | 경기도 고양시 덕양구 통일로 140 삼송테크노밸리 A동 3층 333호
전화 | 02)389-0152
팩스 | 02)389-0156
홈페이지 | www.miraejisig.co.kr
이메일 | miraejisig@naver.com
등록번호 | 제 2018-000205호

*이 책의 판권은 미래지식에 있습니다.
*값은 표지 뒷면에 표기되어 있습니다.
*잘못된 책은 구입하신 서점에서 바꾸어 드립니다.

ISBN 979-11-91349-50-4 64700
ISBN 979-11-90107-41-9 (세트)

*미래주니어는 미래지식의 어린이책 브랜드입니다.